Texas

Bed & Breakfast
Cookbook

Recipes with a

Texas flair shared

by Innkeepers

from B&Bs

Statewide

EXPANDED
2nd edition
New Inns
New Recipes

By Carol Faino
& Erin Faino

"We dedicate this cookbook
to all the warm-hearted, hard-working
Texas bed and breakfast owners,
innkeepers, and chefs,
who took time from their busy schedules
to generously share their favorite recipes.
THANKS, Y'ALL!"
Carol and Erin

9   8   7   6   5   4   3   2

Second Edition
ISBN 978-1-889593-20-3
PUBLISHED BY:
3D Press
a Big Earth Publishing company
3005 Center Green Drive, Suite 220
Boulder, CO 80301

800-258-5830 (order toll free)
303-443-9687 (fax)
www.bigearthpublishing.com

FRONT COVER PHOTO: TOP: Ingleside Bed & Breakfast; **BOTTOM:** Great Oaks Manor
COVER AND TEXT DESIGN: Rebecca Finkel
EDITING: Claire Summerfield, Linda Doyle, Mira Perrizo, Molly Hazelrig
PRINTED IN China by Imago
The Bed & Breakfast Cookbook Series was originated by Carol Faino & Doreen Hazledine of Peppermint Press in Denver, Colorado in 1996.

Texas: The Lone Star State

FAMOUS TEXANS:
Joan Crawford
Tommy Lee Jones
Debbie Reynolds
Steve Martin
Willie Nelson
Howard Hughes
Lance Armstrong
Scott Joplin
A.J. Foyt

THE MOST INFAMOUS TEXAS PAIR:
Bonnie Parker and Clyde Barrow

GEOGRAPHIC FEATURES OF NOTE:
624 miles of coastline
8,751-foot elevation (Guadalupe Peak); highest point
113,400 acres makes Sam Rayburn Reservoir the largest
    body of water in the state
2 National Parks
4 National Forests
2nd largest canyon in the U.S.—Palo Duro Canyon

OFFICIAL STATE SYMBOLS:
STATE BIRD: Mockingbird
STATE INSECT: Monarch Butterfly
STATE FLOWER: Bluebonnet
STATE PLANT: Prickly Pear Cactus
STATE TREE: Pecan
STATE FISH: Guadalupe Bass
STATE FOLK DANCE: Square Dance
STATE SMALL MAMMAL: 9-banded Armadillo

The Official Dish of the State of Texas is Chili con carne, often known simply as chili. The essential ingredients are chili peppers and meat. The most authentic way to make chili is with no beans. Beans are served on the side and added to the chili, if desired. Chili recipes vary from region to region and chili cook offs are a staple at fairs, and community gatherings.

President Lyndon Johnson's favorite chili recipe became known as "Pedernales River chili" after the location of his ranch. First Lady, Lady Bird Johnson cooked the chili with venison when available, avoiding the traditional beef suet. President Johnson had had a heart attack, and orders from his doctor suggested a lower-fat version. The First Lady was swamped with requests and had the recipe printed up on cards as a mailing for an easy, quick reply.

Mrs. Lyndon B. Johnson's recipe for Pedernales River Chili

4 pounds chili meat (coarsely-ground roundsteak
   or well-trimmed chuck)
1 large onion, chopped
2 cloves garlic
1 teaspoon ground oregano
1 teaspoon comino seed
6 teaspoons chili powder (more if desired)
1½ cups canned tomatoes
2–6 generous dashes of liquid hot sauce
   (hot pepper sauce)
2 cups hot water
salt, to taste

Place meat, onion, and garlic in a large heavy pot or dutch oven. Cook until light in color. Add oregano, comino seed, chili powder, tomatoes, hot pepper sauce, salt, and hot water. Bring to a boil. Lower heat and simmer for about 1 hour. Skim off fat during cooking.

Contents

Breads, Pastries, & Granola

Breads, Pastries, & Granola

> "When I am in trouble, eating
> is the only thing that consoles me . . .
> At the present moment I am eating
> muffins because I am unhappy.
> Besides, I am particularly fond
> of muffins."
>
> —OSCAR WILDE

THE COTTON PALACE

Located in a 1910 Arts and Crafts-style house, the Cotton Palace Bed & Breakfast has been completely renovated to showcase the exquisite woodwork and design of Roy Elspeth Lane, Waco's premier architect. The Cotton Palace is a retreat—whether staying for business or pleasure.

Explore the rich heritage of Waco and central Texas, and all it has to offer from the inn's historic address on Austin Avenue.

"A step away from the everyday world ... into a world of friendly and charming hospitality. A place of beauty, peaceful rest and sumptuous food. A wonderful place to restore mind, soul, and body."

— GUEST

INNKEEPERS:	Becky Hodges and Dutch & Betty Schroeder
ADDRESS:	1910 Austin Avenue, Waco, Texas 76701
TELEPHONE:	(254) 753-7294; (877) 632-2312; (254) 753-7921 fax
E-MAIL:	cotnpalace@aol.com
WEBSITE:	www.thecottonpalace.com
ROOMS:	4 Rooms; 2 Suites; 1 Cottage; Private baths
CHILDREN:	Age 12 and older welcome
PETS:	Not allowed

Glazed Cream Cheese Bread

Makes 4 Loaves

Plan ahead – the dough needs to chill overnight before making and baking the bread. This bread freezes well.

1 cup sour cream
½ cup plus ¾ cup sugar
1 teaspoon plus ⅛ teaspoon salt
1 stick (½ cup) butter, melted
2 packages (5 teaspoons) active dry yeast
½ cup warm water (105–115°F)
2 eggs, beaten plus 1 egg, beaten
4 cups flour
2 (8-ounce) packages cream cheese, room temperature
2 teaspoons plus 1 teaspoon vanilla extract
2 cups powdered sugar
¼ cup milk

Heat sour cream in a small saucepan over low heat. Stir in ½ cup sugar, 1 teaspoon salt and butter. Remove from heat and let cool to lukewarm. Sprinkle yeast over warm water in a large mixing bowl; stir to dissolve. Add sour cream mixture, 2 beaten eggs and flour; mix well. Tightly cover dough and chill overnight.

The next day, divide dough into 4 equal portions. On a well-floured surface, roll each portion into a 12x18-inch rectangle. Combine cream cheese, ¾ cup sugar, 1 beaten egg, ⅛ teaspoon salt and 2 teaspoons of vanilla; mix until smooth. Spread ¼ of the cream cheese filling over each rectangle of dough. Beginning at long edge, roll up, jelly-roll style. Pinch seam to seal; tuck ends under. Place rolls, seam-side-down, on greased baking sheets. Cut slits about ⅔ of the way through the dough at 2-inch intervals. Cover and let rise in a warm place (80–85°F) for about 1 hour, or until doubled in size.

Preheat oven to 375°F. Bake for 12–15 minutes. While bread is baking, make a glaze by combining 1 teaspoon vanilla, powdered sugar and milk. Blend until smooth. Spread glaze over warm loaves.

JEFFERSON STREET B&B

Magnificent shade trees are abundant in the calm, quiet neighborhood of the Jefferson Street Bed & Breakfast. Jefferson Street is located in the charming historic district of Irving between Dallas and Ft. Worth. Built in 2006, this ranch-style house has the feel of the early Texas frontier. However, the accessibility of cable television with over one hundred and sixty channels and the fiber optic wireless Internet in the home are definitely benefits of the present century. The whimsical cowboy artifacts add an amusing touch to the décor at the Jefferson Street B&B.

The 1927 Craftsman-style cottage adjacent to the main house is an alternative lodging choice for travelers. Huge elms, oaks, and colorful crepe myrtles surround the cottage that will accommodate up to six people. Continental breakfast fixings are supplied in the cottage kitchen or you may want to saunter over to the ranch house for your morning meal.

Hard surface flooring, environmentally-friendly cleaning products, individual air conditioning units, and the "no pets" and "no smoking" policies at this inn provide a clean, fresh atmosphere for chemically sensitive or allergy prone individuals seeking safe accommodations away from home.

INNKEEPERS:	Tom and Lee Lowrie
ADDRESS:	512 South Jefferson Street, Irving, Texas 75060-4145
TELEPHONE:	(972)-253-2000; (972)-253-2001 fax
E-MAIL:	JeffersonStreetBnB@hotmail.com
WEBSITE:	www.JeffersonStreetBnB.com
ROOMS:	8 Suites; 2 Cottages; Private baths
CHILDREN:	Welcome
PETS:	Not allowed

Bread Machine Bread

Makes 1 Loaf

"Everyone loves this fresh hot bread for breakfast.
To get the best bread, use the freshest ingredients."
—INNKEEPER, Jefferson Street Bed and Breakfast

$\frac{7}{8}$ cup of cold (38°F) fresh milk

3 tablespoons frozen butter

1 grade AA egg, cold (38°F)

1¾ tablespoon sugar

1 teaspoon salt

½ cup bread flour taken directly from the bag
  and lightly packed in measuring cup

1½ cup all-purpose flour, taken directly from the bag
  and lightly packed in measuring cup

¾ teaspoon Fleischmann's Bread Machine yeast, cold (38°F)

Add all ingredients to the bread machine baking can, with the exception of the yeast. The yeast should be put in last into an indentation made in the top of the flour so that it does not get wet before the machine starts. Follow baking directions for your bread machine, using the setting for "light crust white bread." Bread should be done 20 minutes before it is served.

TIPS:

• Bread flour is needed in the mix because it has more gluten than all-purpose flour, and gives body to the bread. The all-purpose flour makes the bread tender, soft and delicious.

• Buy a jar of yeast and keep it in the refrigerator. Foil packets have too much yeast per package for bread machines.

• If your bread does not rise properly, it is probably due to too much milk relative to the flour.

• Don't substitute oil for butter. The bread will lose much of its great taste.

GRUENE APPLE

At the end of a tree-lined lane, on a bluff overlooking the Guadalupe River, you will find the Gruene Apple Bed & Breakfast. With its magnificent limestone exterior, expansive porches and soaring 22-foot-high entrance hall, the Gruene Apple offers a world of unsurpassed elegance and hospitality.

Settle into a wingback swivel chair in the media room to watch a movie on the 12-foot-wide screen. Or, take a refreshing dip in the natural stone swimming pool and hot tub. If you are the active type enjoy a day of tubing on the Guadalupe River.

For nightlife, you won't want to miss dancing at the famous Gruene Hall just a few hundred yards away. Gruene Hall is one of Texas' oldest dance halls.

INNKEEPERS:	Ki, Lloyd & Linda Kleypas
ADDRESS:	1235 Gruene Road, New Braunfels, Texas 78130
TELEPHONE:	(830) 643-1234
E-MAIL:	info@grueneapple.com
WEBSITE:	www.grueneapple.com
ROOMS:	14 Rooms; Private baths
CHILDREN:	Unable to accommodate
PETS:	Not allowed; Resident cats

Pumpkin Coconut Bread

Makes 1 Loaf

2 eggs
1 cup sugar
¾ cup vegetable oil
1½ ups flour
1 teaspoon baking powder
1 teaspoon baking soda
½ teaspoon salt
½ teaspoon nutmeg
½ teaspoon ground ginger
½ teaspoon cinnamon
1 (3½-ounce) package instant coconut cream pudding mix
1 cup canned or cooked mashed pumpkin
½ cup chopped pecans

Preheat oven to 350°F. Spray a 9x5-inch loaf pan with nonstick cooking spray. In a large bowl, beat together eggs, sugar and oil. In a medium bowl, combine flour, baking powder, baking soda, salt, nutmeg, ginger, cinnamon and pudding mix; add dry ingredients to egg mixture. Beat on low speed with a mixer, just until combined. Stir in pumpkin and pecans. Spoon batter into prepared pan.

Bake for 60 minutes, or until a toothpick inserted in the center comes out clean. Cool in pan for 10 minutes. Remove from loaf pan. Cool loaf completely on wire rack.

Knittel Homestead Inn

In Burton, halfway between Houston and Austin, sits the meticulously restored and updated Knittel Homestead Inn. Lodging is provided in The Washington House, a 1914 farmhouse, and the 1870 Knittel House, a two-story Texas Victorian built to look like a Mississippi river boat. The rooms are large and well decorated with

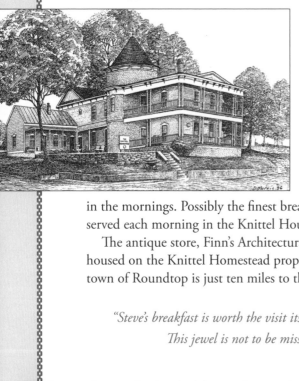

early twentieth-century antiques. Each room has a private bath, a writing desk, a sitting area, individual climate control, a television, and a clock radio.

Complementary snacks and soft drinks are available anytime in the parlor. Fresh, hot coffee and the local newspaper await you in the mornings. Possibly the finest breakfast you've ever eaten is served each morning in the Knittel House dining room.

The antique store, Finn's Architectural and Eclectic Antiques, is housed on the Knittel Homestead property, and the antique lover's town of Roundtop is just ten miles to the west of the inn.

"Steve's breakfast is worth the visit itself—what a masterpiece!!
This jewel is not to be missed!" —Guest

INNKEEPERS: Steve and Carmen Finn
ADDRESS: 520 North Main Street, Burton, Texas 77835
MAILING: PO Box 84, Burton, Texas 77835
TELEPHONE: (979) 289-5102; (979) 289-0067
E-MAIL: stay@knittelhomestead.com
WEBSITE: www.knittelhomestead.com
ROOMS: 6 Rooms; Private baths
CHILDREN: Age 12 and older welcome
PETS: Not allowed; Resident dog

Cheddar Nut Bread

Makes 1 Loaf

"Great right out of the oven and served with butter or cream cheese. Can even be toasted the next day—if there is any left!"
—INNKEEPER, *Knittel Homestead Inn*

1 large egg, slightly beaten
1 cup evaporated milk
½ cup water
¼ teaspoon salt
3¾ cup Buttermilk Baking Mix
1½ cup sharp cheddar cheese, grated
½ cup pecans, chopped

Preheat oven to 350°F. Butter a 9x5x3-inch loaf pan. In a large bowl, combine all ingredients in the order listed. Mix vigorously by hand for 30 seconds or until well-blended. Mixture will be fairly stiff. Spoon into buttered loaf pan and bake for 60 minutes. Serve warm or cold.

BlissWood

The BlissWood Bed & Breakfast is conveniently located in Cat Spring, approximately 60 miles west of Houston. The area around the inn is rich in Texas historical attractions. Guests enjoy exploring the cultural attractions and numerous antique shops in the nearby communities. Bass fishing, trap shooting, archery and golf are also available.

For those who enjoy riding, the innkeeper will saddle up a quarter horse or a gaited Paso Fino from South America and guests can take a leisurely ride across the meadows, through oak forests, across creeks, and past soothing ponds.

The Writer's Cabin is a secluded one-bedroom house hidden back among the oaks. If you need to truly get away, this is a place of perfect seclusion.

INNKEEPER:	Carol Davis
ADDRESS:	13251 Newberg Road, Cat Spring, Texas 78933
TELEPHONE:	(713) 301-3235
E-MAIL:	carol@blisswood.net
WEBSITE:	www.blisswood.net
ROOMS:	8 Cottages; Private baths
CHILDREN:	Call ahead
PETS:	Call ahead; Resident dogs

Blueberry Cornbread Mini-Loaves

Makes 3 Small Loaves

*"Wrap and store these loaves overnight –
they're actually tastier the day after baking."*
—INNKEEPER, *BlissWood*

1½ cups flour
1½ cups yellow cornmeal
¾ cup sugar
1 tablespoon baking powder
½ teaspoon salt
½ teaspoon plus 1 teaspoon finely grated lemon zest
2 eggs, beaten
1¼ cups milk
½ teaspoon vanilla extract
¼ cup vegetable oil (such as canola)
1 cup fresh blueberries (or substitute frozen blueberries)
¾ cup plus 1 tablespoon sifted powdered sugar
2 teaspoons lemon juice
Water or milk (about 2–3 teaspoons)
1 stick (½ cup) butter, room temperature
1 teaspoon lemon zest

Preheat oven to 350°F. Grease bottoms and ½-inch up the sides of 3 small 5x3-inch loaf pans. In a large bowl, combine flour, cornmeal, sugar, baking powder, salt and ½ teaspoon lemon zest. Make a well in center of dry ingredients. In another bowl, combine eggs, milk, vanilla, and oil; add dry ingredients and stir just until moistened. Fold in blueberries. Spoon batter into pans. Bake for 35–40 minutes, or until toothpick inserted in the center comes out clean. Cool in pans on wire racks for 10 minutes. Remove from pans. Cool completely. Wrap loaves tightly and store overnight.

The next day, make a lemon glaze by combining ¾ cup powdered sugar, lemon juice and enough water or milk to reach a drizzling consistency. Make a lemon butter by combining butter, 1 tablespoon powdered sugar and 1 teaspoon lemon zest. Drizzle the loaves with the lemon glaze and serve with lemon butter.

Casa de Siesta

The Casa de Siesta Bed & Breakfast is located on South Padre Island, a coastal resort town on the Gulf of Mexico with five miles of seashore fun, shopping, dining and water activities. The island, bordered by the Laguna Madre Bay, is also ecologically significant with 34 miles of sand dunes, water birds, shrimp and the best deep-sea fishing in Texas. The inn is located just one block from the beach, and one block from the bay.

All the building materials and décor of Casa de Siesta are representative of Mexican, North American and Anglo cultures of the Southwest. The rooms are configured around a courtyard, which historically provided protected open space and was the location of the community well. The "well" is a fountain made in Mexico from a volcanic stone called "cantera." The fountain is hand carved from large blocks of this stone.

INNKEEPERS: Ron and Lynn Speier
ADDRESS: 4610 Padre Boulevard, South Padre Island, Texas 78597
TELEPHONE: (956) 761-5656; (956) 761-1313 fax
E-MAIL: info@casadesiesta.com
WEBSITE: www.casadesiesta.com
ROOMS: 12 Rooms; Private baths
CHILDREN: Age 12 and older welcome
PETS: Welcome

Banana Applesauce Bread

Makes 2 Loaves

*"Save your overripe bananas for this bread (they will last for
a few more days in the refrigerator, or they can also be frozen,
if you are not quite ready to make this delicious bread)."*
—INNKEEPER, *Casa de Siesta*

1 stick (½ cup) butter, room temperature
1½ cups sugar
2 eggs
3–4 very ripe bananas, chopped into
    small pieces (about 2 cups)
½ cup applesauce
2 cups flour
1 teaspoon baking soda
¼ teaspoon salt
1 cup chopped walnuts

Preheat oven to 325°F. Grease and flour 2 9x5-inch loaf pans.
In a large bowl, cream together butter and sugar; add eggs, bananas
and applesauce; beat on low speed with a mixer until well combined.
Sift together flour, baking soda and salt; add to wet ingredients;
mix well. Stir in nuts. Divide mixture between loaf pans (pans
will be slightly less than ½-full).

Bake for 50–55 minutes, or until a toothpick inserted in the center
comes out clean. Let loaves cool in the pans on a wire rack for
10 minutes. Turn loaves out. Bread may be served warm, or cooled
completely for later use. Slice and serve on a doily-lined plate.

Munzesheimer Manor

At the Munzesheimer Manor, you can sip lemonade on the wrap-around porches, sleep in custom Victorian nightgowns and nightshirts, bathe in a turn-of-the-century, claw-foot tub (with your own rubber ducky) or treat yourself to a bubble bath with therapeutic bath salts.

The Engineer's Room is decorated in a railroad theme, complete with the "dead man's clutch," large caboose lamp and other relics of Mineola's historic connection to the railroad, which dates back to 1873.

The Tack Room is built on the site of the stable and is the most private of all the rooms. Lumber from an old house being demolished down the street was used for the floor-to-ceiling bookshelves and one of the walls.

INNKEEPERS: Bob and Sherry Murray

ADDRESS: 202 North Newsom, Mineola, Texas 75773

TELEPHONE: (903) 569-6634; (888) 569-6634; (903) 569-9940 fax

E-MAIL: innkeeper@munzesheimer.com

WEBSITE: www.munzesheimer.com

ROOMS: 4 Rooms; 3 Cottages; Private baths

CHILDREN: Welcome; Call ahead

PETS: Not allowed; Resident dog

Morning Glory Mini-Muffins

Makes 4 Dozen Mini-Muffins

*"This batter can be made in advance and frozen in the muffin pans.
Thaw overnight in the refrigerator when ready to use."*
—INNKEEPER, *Munzesheimer Manor*

2 cups flour
1 cup sugar
2 teaspoons baking soda
2 teaspoons cinnamon
1 apple, peeled, cored and grated
½ cup raisins
½ cup shredded coconut
½ cup pecans, chopped
1 cup carrots, grated
3 eggs
½ cup vegetable oil
1 stick (½ cup) butter, melted
2 teaspoons vanilla extract

Preheat oven to 350°F. Spray mini-muffin cups with nonstick
cooking spray. In a large bowl, sift together flour, sugar, baking
soda, and cinnamon. Add grated apple, raisins, coconut, pecans,
and grated carrots. Mix thoroughly, until mixture resembles a
coarse meal.

In a medium bowl, beat eggs with a whisk. Add oil, butter and
vanilla; whisk to blend. Add wet ingredients to dry ingredients;
stir just until combined. Spoon batter into muffin cups. (At this
point, the batter can be covered and frozen.) Bake for 10–12 minutes,
or until done. Cool for 5 minutes before removing muffins from
muffin pans. Serve warm.

ROCKIN RIVER INN

The Rockin River Inn is surrounded by Hill Country native landscapes that display a Texas wildflower show in the spring and a spectacular changing of the leaves in the fall. A full gourmet breakfast includes farm-raised eggs and home-baked pastries. The inn has a swimming pool and offers hunting packages and bike trail maps.

The Rockin River Inn is constructed of long-leaf pine floors, 20-inch-thick walls and hammered brass door hardware, and boasts a native-stone fireplace.

The entire facility can be rented for weddings, reunions and corporate retreats.

INNKEEPER:	Ken Wardlaw
ADDRESS:	103 Skyline Road, Center Point, Texas 78010
TELEPHONE:	(830) 634-7043; (866) 424-0576
E-MAIL:	relax@rockinriverinn.com
WEBSITE:	www.rockinriverinn.com
ROOMS:	3 Rooms; 1 Suite; Private baths
CHILDREN:	Welcome
PETS:	Not allowed; Resident dog

Fredericksburg Peach Muffins

Makes 12 Muffins

*"I created this muffin recipe to take advantage of the big,
juicy peaches grown all around Fredericksburg and Stonewall.
When the short summer peach season is over,
you can substitute good quality frozen peaches—and only
those who live in the Hill Country will know the difference."*
—INNKEEPER, *Rockin River Inn*

1 cup flour
1 teaspoon baking powder
½ teaspoon baking soda
¼ teaspoon salt
2 eggs
1 cup premium whole milk yogurt
    (do not use low-fat or non-fat)
¾ cup brown sugar, packed
1 cup quick-cooking or old-fashioned rolled oats
⅓ cup butter, melted
½ teaspoon lemon extract
1 teaspoon lemon zest, grated
1 cup peaches, peeled, chopped (½-inch cubes)
¾ cup walnuts, finely chopped

Preheat oven to 350°F. Spray 12 muffin cups with nonstick cooking
spray. In a medium bowl, combine flour, baking powder, baking
soda and salt; make a well in the center.

In another bowl, combine eggs, yogurt, brown sugar, oats, melted
butter, lemon extract and lemon zest; add to dry ingredients and
stir just until moistened. Add peaches and walnuts; stir gently just
until combined. Fill muffin cups ¾ full.

Bake for 20–22 minutes on center rack of oven, or until the center
of each muffin springs back when lightly pressed. Cool for 5 minutes
in muffin cups before removing muffins to a wire rack.

LONESOME DOVE

"Where Life Is Simple and the Fragrance of Nature is Free"

Secluded on the grounds of a forty-one-acre ranch and nestled in the woods overlooking a peaceful three-acre pond is the 1850 log cabin called Lonesome Dove. The two-story cabin is perched

on a foundation created from native stone. The wraparound front porch displays a twig loveseat and chair that beckon one to come sit a while. The interior of Lonesome Dove is comfortably furnished with rustic antiques and an abundance of candles.

There is a king-size log bed upstairs, a queen-size sleeper sofa downstairs, a kitchenette, and a claw foot tub in the bathroom. Breakfast is delivered to your door in a basket.

If you venture out of the snug and serene cabin to explore the pond, a canoe and fishing gear will be provided for you at no extra charge. On the grounds beyond the pond, you're welcome to hike the wooded pathways, observe the wildlife, and follow the footbridge to a quiet meditation garden. Lake Somerville Rocky Creek Park is two miles down the road. Lonesome Dove is fifteen miles from the nearest town of Brenham, and Roundtop is twenty-one miles from the cabin.

INNKEEPERS: John and Gay Barnette

ADDRESS: 4421 Rehburg Road, Burton, Texas 77835

TELEPHONE: (979) 289-5005; (979) 289-5045; (979) 830-5849 cell
(979) 289-9011 fax

E-MAIL: stay@lonesomedovebedandbreakfast.com

WEBSITE: www.lonesomedovebedandbreakfast.com

ROOMS: 1 Log Cabin; Private bath

CHILDREN: Welcome

PETS: Not allowed; Resident horses, cats, and a variety of doves, exotic chickens, pigeons and pheasants

Crunchy Granola Muffins

Makes 2 Dozen Muffins

2 cups granola
1 cup flour
1 cup brown sugar
1 teaspoon soda
½ teaspoon salt
1 tablespoon cinnamon
1 stick of butter, melted
2 eggs
1 cup pecans, chopped
1 cup dried cranberries
1 cup raisins

Preheat oven to 350°F. Spray muffin tin with nonstick cooking spray. In a large bowl, mix the first 6 ingredients. Add butter and eggs. Mix well. Add pecans, cranberries, and raisins. Fill muffin cups ¾ full and bake for 15–18 minutes.

All sorrows are less with bread.

—MIQUEL DE CERVANTES,
DON QUIXOTE

GRUENE MANSION INN

The Gruene Mansion Inn has captured the drama and historical flair of Henry D. Gruene's Victorian home in this award-winning bed and breakfast. Not only is the property listed on the National Register of Historic Places, but it is also designated a Texas Historic Landmark. Why stay in a hotel when you can sleep in Texas history?

Such notable musicians as Jerry Jeff Walker, Lyle Lovett, Willie Nelson, the Dixie Chicks and George Strait have all held center stage at the adjacent Gruene Hall, "the oldest dance hall in Texas."

The inn also offers customized "baskets" that add extra fun to your stay. The most popular are: the Texas Romance basket, the Honeymooner's basket and the Guadalupe River basket—great for taking with you down to the river bank.

INNKEEPERS:	Cecil and Judi Eager
ADDRESS:	1275 Gruene Road, New Braunfels, Texas 78130
TELEPHONE:	(830) 629-2641
E-MAIL:	frontdesk@gruenemansioninn.com
WEBSITE:	www.gruenemansioninn.com
ROOMS:	30 Rooms; 12 Suites; 1 Cottage; Private baths
CHILDREN:	Welcome
PETS:	Not allowed

White Chocolate Apricot Muffins

Makes 12 Muffins

*"These flavorful muffins are good with or without
the crystallized ginger."*
—INNKEEPER, *Gruene Mansion Inn*

1¼ cups flour
½ cup plus 2 tablespoons sugar
1½ teaspoons baking powder
½ teaspoon salt
1 tablespoon minced crystallized ginger
2 (1-ounce) squares white baking chocolate,
    finely chopped
¾ cup 1% milk
3 tablespoons butter, melted
1 large egg, lightly beaten
½ cup apricot preserves

Preheat oven to 400°F. Spray 12 muffin cups with nonstick cooking
spray. In a large bowl, combine flour, ½ cup sugar, baking powder,
salt, crystallized ginger, and chopped white chocolate. Make a
well in the center. In a small bowl, combine milk, melted butter
and egg; add to the dry ingredients and stir until just combined.

Spoon 1 tablespoon of batter into each muffin cup. Put about
1¼ teaspoons of apricot preserves in the center of the batter in
each muffin cup. Top with 1 tablespoon of batter. Sprinkle each
muffin with ½ teaspoon sugar. Bake for 20–22 minutes. Cool for
5 minutes in the muffin pan on a wire rack. Remove from pan.
Serve warm, or cool for later use.

Mt. Gainor Inn

Panoramic sunrises and sunsets and serene ranchland views surround the twenty-three hilltop acres of the Mt. Gainor Inn. The paths and scenic back roads winding though the countryside provide opportunities for cycling enthusiasts and wildlife watchers. Mt. Gainor Inn is an early twentieth-century German farmhouse

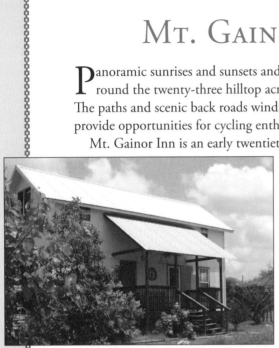

located in the Central Texas Wine District. Each suite in the bed and breakfast has its own private entrance. The Garden Room is filled with plants and natural light and boasts an incredible Hill Country view. A covered deck and two-person whirlpool bath enhance the ambiance of The Hideaway.

The fireplace in the Attic Suite is the essential romantic element. The decks are an extension of the living space featuring comfortable rocking chairs, ceiling fans, and conversation nooks.

A full breakfast is provided daily and a gourmet dinner is served family-style in the dining room or the honeysuckle and jasmine covered pavilion.

"Ya'll put the breakfast back in bed and breakfast. The food was incredible and the hospitality was true Texan." — Guest

INNKEEPERS:	Laurie and Jerry Pinnix
ADDRESS:	2390 Prochnow Road, Dripping Springs, Texas 78620
MAILING:	(2380 Prochnow Road) 78620
TELEPHONE:	(512) 858-0982; (888) 644-0982
E-MAIL:	laurie@mtgainorinn.com
WEBSITE:	www.mtgainorinn.com
ROOMS:	2 Rooms; 1 Suite; Private baths
CHILDREN:	Age 12 and older are welcome
PETS:	Not allowed

Jam-Filled Muffins

Makes 12 Muffins

"I use several different jams, so my guests never know which flavor they will get. This is a fun recipe to play with. Our guests are always happily surprised and ask for another one."
—INNKEEPER, *Mt. Gainor Inn*

2 cups all-purpose flour
¾ cup sugar
1 tablespoon baking powder
½ teaspoon baking soda
½ teaspoon salt
6 tablespoons unsalted butter, melted
2 large eggs
1 teaspoon vanilla extract, (prefer Mexican vanilla)
¼ teaspoon almond extract
1¼ cups sour cream
$^1/_3$–½ cup seedless jam (choose your favorite)

Preheat oven to 375°F. Grease 12 standard muffin cups with butter or butter-flavored cooking spray. In a large bowl, stir together flour, sugar, baking powder, baking soda, and salt. In a small bowl, whisk together melted butter, eggs, vanilla, almond extract, and sour cream until smooth. Add egg mixture to dry ingredients; stir until evenly mixed. The batter will be slightly lumpy. Do not over mix. Spoon batter into muffin cups; filling ⅓-full. Drop a heaping spoonful of jam into the center; cover with additional batter; fill to the rim.

Bake 20–25 minutes until muffins are golden and spring to the touch. Transfer pan to rack and let cool for 5 minutes. Serve warm or at room temperature..

Brazos B&B

"Where the Brazos River meets up with the History of Texas"

Situated on ten rolling acres, Brazos Bed and Breakfast is in the town of Washington, just two miles from the birthplace of Texas. Follow the winding road from the inn to the secluded grove of lush, live oaks and you will discover one of the most serene spots in Washington County.

Two exceptional suites are offered at the Brazos. Both suites include a butler's pantry, Dish TV, wireless Internet service, and a full bathroom. Enter the enchanting Tree Top Suite from your private balcony and outdoor dining area. The roomy Texan Suite extends outdoors onto a large back patio complete with a romantic arbor, a fire pit, a gas grill, and a view of the organic garden. After you have had a wonderful night's sleep on Egyptian cotton sheets, your morning begins with a generous breakfast delivered to your door in a basket.

"Wow! What an awesome experience! I came here with my mother but I'll be back with my husband!" —GUEST

INNKEEPER:	Diane Hunter
ADDRESS:	20251 Pickens Road, Washington, Texas 77880
TELEPHONE:	(936) 878-2230 phone and fax
E-MAIL:	dianebrazosbb@sbcglobal.net
WEBSITE:	www. brazosbedandbreakfast.com
ROOMS:	2 Suites; Private baths
CHILDREN:	Unable to accommodate
PETS:	Not allowed; Resident chickens and cows

Blueberry Bran Muffins

Makes 4 Dozen Muffins

*"Our guests love this blueberry bran muffin,
and often comment on its texture and delicious flavor.
They are wonderfully fresh-tasting right from the freezer."*
—INNKEEPER, *Brazos Bed and Breakfast*

3½ cups sugar, divided
4 eggs, lightly beaten
1 quart low fat buttermilk
1 cup canola oil
1 tablespoon baking soda
2 teaspoons baking powder
2 teaspoons salt
5 cups flour
15 ounces of Bran Flake cereal
2 cups blueberries, fresh or frozen

Preheat oven to 400°F. Spray muffin pan with nonstick cooking spray. In a large bowl, mix sugar, eggs, buttermilk, and oil. In a separate bowl, whisk together baking soda, baking powder, salt, and flour. When mixed well, stir in bran flakes. Add to wet ingredients. In a small bowl, toss ½ cup sugar with blueberries.

Fill muffin cups ⅛ full with mixture. Add the blueberries to the remaining mixture and continue to fill muffin cups to ¾ full. Bake for 15–20 minutes.

AMERICAN HERITAGE HOUSE

This spectacular Federal-style mansion is quietly positioned in the lush Brazos River Valley in the northern Texas town of Granbury. The innkeepers at American Heritage House welcome you through the nineteenth-century doorway into a Texas Bed and Breakfast clearly beyond the ordinary. The 1,630-square-foot wrap around porch allows ample room for daydreams to take flight. A piano in the music room is available for melodious guests and a sixty-five-inch theatre screen complete with a DVD library offers the opportunity to escape and be entertained. Putters and golf balls are provided for the on-site putting green.

Each of the six boutique bedrooms and the three cottages are enchantingly unique. All guests are treated to a multi-course gourmet sit-down breakfast fit for royalty. The meal is served on fine china and crystal in the formal dining room. The American Heritage House event facility can accommodate up to sixty people and is just the right size for corporate retreats.

INNKEEPERS: Ron and Karen Bleeker

ADDRESS: 225 West Moore Street, Granbury, Texas 76048

TELEPHONE: (817) 578-3768; (866) 778-3768

E-MAIL: info@americanheritagehouse.com

WEBSITE: www.americanheritagehouse.com

ROOMS: 4 Rooms; 2 Suites; 3 Cottages

CHILDREN: Welcome in the cottages;
Age 12 and older in the main house

PETS: Not allowed

Heritage House
Signature Pecan Pie Muffins

Makes 24 Mini-Muffins

1 cup light brown sugar, packed
1 cup flour
¾ cup pecans, chopped
1 egg
1 stick butter, melted

Preheat oven to 325°F. Spray mini-muffin pan with a nonstick cooking spray. In a large bowl, combine brown sugar, flour, and pecans; add egg and butter. Combine until all ingredients are moistened. Spoon mixture into muffin pan. Bake for 18 minutes or until edges are just turning brown. Do not over cook or they will be hard. Let stand 10 minutes in muffin pan.

TIP:
- If you try to remove them in less than 10 minutes, they will not hold their shape. If you wait longer, they won't pop out easily.

WISTERIA HIDEAWAY

G uests are invited to a full breakfast at Wisteria Hideaway Bed & Breakfast. Breakfast meats are custom processed, providing a flavorful accompaniment to dishes that vary from creamy scrambled eggs and frittatas to spicy egg casseroles. Buttermilk biscuits baked to a tender crust in an iron skillet, or sweet potato muffins go nicely with the inn's homemade jellies.

The dining room features original wall coverings and full-length windows.

Wisteria Hideaway is the ideal location to make your wedding day a cherished memory. The four-acre estate offers heirloom gardens, rich green lawns and beautiful arbors. The majestic oaks and the abundance of age-old wisteria provide a beauty that will enhance the elegance of your wedding.

INNKEEPERS:	Ron and Brenda A.Cole
ADDRESS:	3458 Ted Trout Drive, Lufkin, Texas 75904
TELEPHONE:	(936) 875-2914; (936) 875-2915
E-MAIL:	info@wisteriahideaway.com
WEBSITE:	www.wisteriahideaway.com
ROOMS:	3 Rooms; 1 Suite; Private baths
CHILDREN:	Welcome
PETS:	Not allowed; Resident outdoor cat

Sweet Potato Muffins

Makes 12 Muffins

*"For these muffins, I bake sweet potatoes,
then cool and freeze them until ready to use.
I feel they have better flavor than boiled sweet potatoes."*
—INNKEEPER, *Wisteria Hideaway*

1½ cups flour
¾ cup sugar
¾ teaspoon baking powder
½ teaspoon baking soda
½ teaspoon cinnamon
½ teaspoon salt
¼ cup vegetable oil
¼ cup water
2 eggs, slightly beaten
¾ cup cooked, mashed sweet potato
(may also use drained canned sweet potatoes)

Preheat oven to 400°F. Spray 12 muffin cups with nonstick cooking spray. In a large bowl, combine flour, sugar, baking powder, baking soda, cinnamon, and salt. In a small bowl, combine oil, water, eggs, and sweet potatoes. Add wet ingredients to dry ingredients; stir just until moistened. Spoon batter into muffin cups.

Bake for 20 minutes, or until a toothpick inserted in the center comes out clean. Cool in pan on a wire rack for 5 minutes. Serve warm.

ROSEVINE INN

The Rosevine Inn Bed & Breakfast is conveniently located in Tyler, with numerous antique and craft shops only a short distance away. Visitors can explore Dewberry Plantation, East Texas Symphony Orchestra Association, Tiger Creek Wildlife Refuge, and the Tyler Rose Museum.

The Lodge Room is modeled after a room in a museum in Strasbourg, France. It is intimate and refined, yet rustic and quaint. A queen-size bed is nestled into one alcove, while a six-foot soaking tub is tucked into another.

INNKEEPERS:	Rebecca and Bert Powell
ADDRESS:	415 South Vine, Tyler, Texas 75702
TELEPHONE:	(903) 592-2221; (903) 592-5522
E-MAIL:	info@rosevine.com
WEBSITE:	www.rosevine.com
ROOMS:	6 Rooms; 1 Suite; 2 Cottages; Private baths
CHILDREN:	Age 5 and older welcome
PETS:	Not allowed; Resident outdoor cats

Fresh Apple Coffee Cake

Makes 10 to 12 Servings

"Thelma, a lady who worked for my grandmother for years, gave me this recipe. I think of her every time I make it."
— INNKEEPER, *Rosevine Inn*

3 cups flour
1½ teaspoons baking soda
½ teaspoon nutmeg
½ teaspoon cinnamon
½ teaspoon salt
2 cups sugar
1½ cups vegetable oil
2 eggs
3 cups Granny Smith apples, peeled, chopped
1 cup pecans, chopped
1½ cups powdered sugar, sifted
1 tablespoon butter, melted
1 tablespoon lemon juice
Water (about 3–4 teaspoons)

Preheat oven to 350°F. Spray a 9-10-inch spring form pan or a 12-cup Bundt pan with nonstick cooking spray. In a large bowl, sift together flour, baking soda, nutmeg, cinnamon, and salt. Make a well in the center of the dry ingredients; set aside. In a medium bowl, combine sugar, oil and eggs; add to dry ingredients, stirring to combine (the batter will be thick). Stir in apples and pecans. Spoon batter into baking pan.

Bake for 60 minutes, or until a toothpick inserted in the center comes out clean. Cool cake in pan for 20 minutes. If using a spring form pan, remove the sides of the pan after 20 minutes. If using a Bundt pan, remove the cake from the pan after 20 minutes. Finish cooling the cake on a wire rack.

While cake is cooling, make a lemon glaze by combining powdered sugar, melted butter and lemon juice in a small bowl. Stir in enough water to reach a drizzling consistency. When cake has completely cooled, drizzle with the lemon glaze.

A BECKMANN INN
AND CARRIAGE HOUSE

Located in downtown San Antonio, Texas across the street from the beautifully landscaped River Walk and minutes to the Alamo by trolley, this inn is the perfect location for business or leisure travel. It is listed in the National Register of Historic places, King William Historic District, San Antonio, Texas, as an "exceptional" City Historic

Landmark. The house was built in 1886 by Albert Beckmann for his bride, Marie Dorothea, daughter of the Guenther Flour Mill family, on the mill grounds. The property was given to Albert and Marie Dorothea as a wedding gift.

The wonderful wrap-around porch warmly welcomes guests through the rare burl pine door to the main house. The inn allows guests to experience Victorian hospitality in a quiet and tranquil atmosphere.

The wicker furniture on the sun porch invites guests to relax and enjoy the "welcome tea," which includes complimentary chocolates and butter cookies.

INNKEEPER:	Charles Stallcup
ADDRESS:	222 East Guenther Street, San Antonio, Texas 78204
TELEPHONE:	(210) 229-1449; (800) 945-1449
E-MAIL:	stay@beckmanninn.com
WEBSITE:	www.beckmanninn.com
ROOMS:	5 Rooms; Private baths
CHILDREN:	Age 12 and older welcome
PETS:	Not allowed

Rhubarb Crumb Coffee Cake

Makes 12 Servings

BATTER:
2 cups flour
1½ cups sugar
2 tablespoons baking powder
1½ sticks (¾ cup) butter, melted
2 eggs
1 cup milk

RHUBARB MIXTURE:
2 cups sliced fresh rhubarb
1 cup sugar
3 tablespoons flour

CRUMB TOPPING:
2 tablespoons flour
2 tablespoons sugar
2 tablespoons butter, chilled

For the batter: Preheat oven to 350°F. Spray a 9x13-inch baking pan with nonstick cooking spray. In a medium bowl, mix flour, sugar, baking powder, and melted butter. Add eggs and milk; stir until combined. Pour batter into the pan.

For the rhubarb mixture: In a large bowl, combine rhubarb, sugar and flour; spoon evenly over the batter in the pan.

For the crumb topping: In a small bowl, combine flour, sugar, and butter. Using a fork or your fingers, mix until crumbly; sprinkle over the rhubarb.

Bake for 45–55 minutes, or until a toothpick inserted in the center comes out clean. Cool on a wire rack.

A YELLOW ROSE

Prepare to be pampered during your stay at A Yellow Rose Bed &
Breakfast. This beautiful 130-year-old Victorian is located in the
King William Historic District in downtown San Antonio. Relax
in spacious guest rooms with luxurious amenities such as Godiva
Chocolates and Caswell Massey bath products.

After breakfast, enjoy a day of strolling on the River Walk, do a
little shopping or take in an exhibit at one of the many museums in
the area.

*"We stayed here for a quick getaway to celebrate our
two-year anniversary. Our room was larger than expected, with a spacious separate bathroom. The location couldn't
be beat ... I have stayed at a number of bed and breakfasts
and this one is my favorite."* — GUEST

INNKEEPERS: Deb and Kit Walker

ADDRESS: 229 Madison, San Antonio, Texas 78204

TELEPHONE: (210) 229-9903; (800) 950-9903

E-MAIL: yellowrose@ddc.net

WEBSITE: www.ayellowrose.com

ROOMS: 5 Rooms; 1 Suite; Private baths

CHILDREN: Age 12 and older welcome

PETS: Not allowed

Buttermilk Scone for Two

Makes 2 Servings

Plan ahead—this large scone takes 30 minutes to bake.

1 cup flour
1½ tablespoons sugar
1 teaspoon baking powder
$\frac{1}{8}$ teaspoon baking soda
½ stick (¼ cup) butter,
    chilled and cut into small pieces
3 tablespoons currants
¼ teaspoon orange zest, grated
¼ cup buttermilk, more if needed
Cinnamon-sugar
    $\frac{1}{8}$ teaspoon cinnamon mixed
    with ½ teaspoon sugar)
Butter and jam, for serving

Preheat oven to 375°F. Grease an 8-to 9-inch round cake or pie
pan. In a medium bowl, sift together flour, sugar, baking powder,
and baking soda. Add butter pieces to dry ingredients; rub with
your fingers to form fine crumbs. Stir in currants and orange zest.
Make a well in the center of the flour mixture; pour in the buttermilk and stir with a fork until dough holds together (add up to
2 more tablespoons of buttermilk, if needed for dough to hold
together).

Pat dough into a ball and knead on a lightly floured surface,
about 5 to 6 times. Shape dough into a smooth ball and place
into greased cake or pie pan. Sprinkle with cinnamon-sugar.

Bake for 10 minutes. Remove from oven and, with a sharp knife,
quickly cut a cross-shape, ½-inch deep, across the top of the scone.
Return the scone to the oven and bake for about 20 minutes more,
or until golden brown. Serve warm with butter and jam.

GREEN GABLES

Come enjoy the amenities of this bed and breakfast hideaway on the Little Blanco River in the beautiful Texas Hill Country. Located on a secluded, private 14-acre estate, Green Gables Bed & Breakfast provides an escape from city noise, ringing telephones and the bustle of everyday life.

Relax beneath the centuries-old pecan and cypress trees that nestle along the banks of the crystal-clear, spring-fed waters of the Little Blanco.

If you prefer to indulge in some tourist activities, you might enjoy shopping the antique and gift stores in Blanco Town Square, touring the 1865 Historic County Courthouse, or taking a drive along the scenic Willow City Loop.

INNKEEPERS: Glen and Sue McFarlin
ADDRESS: 401 Green Gables, Blanco, Texas 78606
TELEPHONE: (830) 833-5931; (888) 833-5931; (830) 833-5944 fax
E-MAIL: info@greengables-tx.com
WEBSITE: www.greengables-tx.com
ROOMS: 1 Suite; 2 Cottages; Private baths
CHILDREN: Welcome
PETS: Not allowed; Resident dogs & cats

Aunt Dora's
Apricot Currant Scones

Makes 8 Scones

"Fresh breads made from scratch are the mainstay of our breakfasts. These scones are a favorite with our guests."
—INNKEEPER, *Green Gables*

2 cups flour
3 tablespoons sugar
½ teaspoon salt
1 tablespoon baking powder
1 stick (½ cup) butter,
    chilled and cut into small pieces
¼ cup currants
¼ cup apricots, chopped
$^{2}/_{3}$ cup milk
1 egg, beaten
Butter, for serving
Jam, for serving

Preheat oven to 400°F. Lightly butter a 9x13-inch baking sheet (if not nonstick). In a medium bowl, combine flour, sugar, salt, and baking powder. Add butter; mix with your fingers to combine and form a soft crumble. Stir in currants and apricots. Add milk; stir just until a soft dough is formed.

Turn dough out onto a floured surface. With lightly floured hands, knead a couple of times to form a loose ball; pat out on the baking sheet into an 8-inch circle. Using a floured, serrated knife, cut the dough into 8 wedges. Wiggle the knife back and forth to separate the edges so that air can circulate between the scones. Brush the tops of the scones with beaten egg.

Bake for 18–20 minutes, or until golden brown and cooked through. Cool on a wire rack for about 5 minutes. Serve warm with butter and jam.

LAKEHOUSE B&B

"Lakehouse Bed and Breakfast was my childhood home.
My family relocated to Canyon Lake in the late 70s
and it was here that I learned to swim, fish, and water ski.
It was after meeting my wife that we decided to pursue
our dream of owning a bed & breakfast."

—INNKEEPER

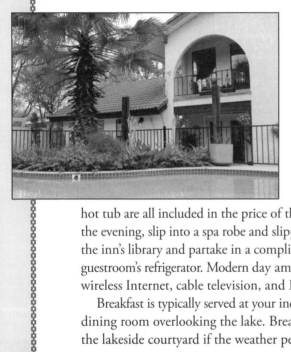

An unobstructed view of Canyon Lake can be seen from this contemporary Mediterranean-style inn near New Braunfels in the Texas Hill Country. The luxuries of a stroll along the shoreline at sunrise, an afternoon lounging next to the sparkling blue pool, or stargazing from the vine-draped hot tub are all included in the price of the room at the Lakehouse. In the evening, slip into a spa robe and slippers, delve into a book from the inn's library and partake in a compli-mentary beverage from your guestroom's refrigerator. Modern day amenities include high-speed wireless Internet, cable television, and DVD and CD players.

Breakfast is typically served at your individual private table in the dining room overlooking the lake. Breakfast can also be enjoyed in the lakeside courtyard if the weather permits.

INNKEEPERS: Justin and Jean Robinson
ADDRESS: 1519 Glenn Drive, Canyon Lake, Texas 78133
TELEPHONE: (830) 899-5099; (866) 616-5253
E-MAIL: questions@thelakehousebb.com
WEBSITE: www.thelakehousebb.com
ROOMS: 2 Rooms; 2 Suites; 2 Cottages; Private baths
CHILDREN: Age 12 and older welcome
PETS: Not allowed

Orange-Almond Scones

Makes 16 Scones

"This is our most requested recipe."
—INNKEEPER, *Lakehouse Bed and Breakfast*

BATTER:

2 cups flour	½ cup orange juice
⅓ cup sugar	1 large egg
1½ teaspoons baking powder	1½ teaspoons almond extract
½ teaspoon baking soda	Zest of ½ orange
1 stick butter	¼ cup almonds, sliced

ORANGE-ALMOND GLAZE:

5 tablespoons powdered sugar	1 teaspoon almond extract
1 tablespoon orange juice	Zest of ½ orange

For the batter: Preheat oven to 400°. In a large bowl, sift together flour, sugar, baking powder, and baking soda. Cut butter into ½-inch cubes and distribute over flour mixture. Cut in the butter with a pastry blender until mixture resembles coarse crumbs. In a small bowl, combine orange juice, egg, almond extract, and orange zest. Add to flour mixture. Add almonds; stir until mixed well. With lightly floured hands, pat the dough into an 8-inch diameter circle on an ungreased cookie sheet. If the dough is sticky, add more flour. Cut into wedges with a serrated knife. Bake 14–16 minutes.

For the glaze: In a small bowl, add orange juice and almond extract to powdered sugar. Stir until blended. Add orange zest. If mixture is too runny, add more sugar; if too thick, add more orange juice. Serve over warm scones.

VARIATIONS:
For Lemon-Poppyseed Scones substitute orange juice for milk; almond extract for lemon extract; sliced almonds for poppy seeds; orange zest for lemon zest.

For Orange-Cranberry Scones substitute almond extract for orange extract; sliced almonds for cranberries.

THE CARLETON HOUSE

Located in the heart of historic downtown Bonham, just one hour northeast of Dallas, is the historic Carleton House Bed & Breakfast. The house was built in 1888 by A.J. Clendenen, who operated a grocery on the square. In 1914, Dr. J.C. Carleton purchased the home for his family and had the house wired for electricity.

This newly renovated three story Victorian, listed on the National Register of Historic Homes, features a large entrance hall, a parlor, dining room with ceiling murals, a music room, breakfast area and a large staircase leading to the bedrooms.

Lillian's Room overlooks the gardens and features a king-size bed, antiques, quilts, and lacy touches for the romantic.

The home, sitting on a landscaped half-acre with remnants of its original gardens is also an ideal setting for weddings and parties.

INNKEEPERS:	Karen and Steve Halbrook
ADDRESS:	803 North Main, Bonham, Texas 75418
TELEPHONE:	(903) 583-2779; (800) 382-8033
E-MAIL:	info@carletonhouse.com
WEBSITE:	www.carletonhouse.com
ROOMS:	5 Rooms; 1 Suite; Private baths
CHILDREN:	Welcome
PETS:	Call ahead

Apricot Cinnamon Scones

Makes 10 Small Scones

BATTER:

1½ cups flour	1 egg
1½ teaspoons baking powder	¾ cup buttermilk
⅛ teaspoon baking soda	¼ cup dried apricots, chopped
½ teaspoon salt	¼ cup cinnamon chips
1 tablespoon sugar	2 tablespoons butter, melted
3 tablespoons shortening	

GLAZE:

½ cup powdered sugar	Dash of cinnamon (optional)
½ teaspoon vanilla extract	1–2 teaspoons water or milk

For the batter: Preheat oven to 400°F. Lightly spray an 8-inch pie pan or round baking pan with nonstick cooking spray. In a large bowl, sift flour, baking powder, baking soda, salt, and sugar. Cut in shortening with a pastry cutter until mixture resembles coarse crumbs; make a well in the center. In a small bowl, whisk egg until light in color; add buttermilk; mix well. Add all at once to the dry ingredients. Using a fork, stir just until moistened (dough will be sticky). Let stand for 5 minutes. Gently stir in apricots and cinnamon chips.

Spoon about ¼ cup of dough onto a floured surface; lightly dust dough with flour. With floured hands, shape into an elongated wedge. Shake off excess flour. Place wedge into pan with the point toward the center. Repeat until all the dough is used and you have created a circle of scones (they will be touching). Brush tops of scones with melted butter. Bake for 15–20 minutes, or until golden brown. Remove from pan and let cool for 10 minutes on a wire rack.

For the glaze: In a small bowl, combine powdered sugar, vanilla, cinnamon, and enough water or milk to reach a drizzling consistency. Stir until smooth; drizzle on slightly cooled scones. Serve warm with jam or jelly.

The Lodges
at Lost Maples

All of the cabins at The Lodges at Lost Maples have hardwood flooring, spacious cathedral ceilings and a quaint living room. Whether you've spent the day hiking at Lost Maples State Natural Area, tubing the Frio or horseback riding in the hills, you'll be glad to kick back in a hammock and enjoy the Hill Country sunset. Each morning, you will awaken to freshly baked breakfast treats such as apricot-white chocolate scones, pecan twists or The Lodge's special rustic warm-center chocolate muffins.

"Very peaceful and relaxing. Certainly wished
we could have stayed longer! Great hospitality!
And the lightning bugs were an added bonus!" —Guest

INNKEEPERS:	The Hathorn Family
ADDRESS:	Ranch Road 337, Vanderpool, Texas 78885
MAILING:	(PO Box 215) 78885
TELEPHONE:	(830) 966-5178; (877) 216-5627
E-MAIL:	lodges@lostmaplescabins.com
WEBSITE:	www.lostmaplescabins.com
ROOMS:	5 Cabins; Private baths
CHILDREN:	Welcome
PETS:	Not allowed

Almost Sinful Cinnamon Rolls

Makes 12 Rolls

"Something this easy shouldn't be this good!"
—INNKEEPER, *The Lodges at Lost Maples*

DOUGH:
2 cups flour
2 tablespoons sugar
4 teaspoons baking powder
1 teaspoon salt
½ stick (¼ cup) butter, chilled
1 cup milk, chilled

FILLING:
⅓ cup butter, softened
1 cup packed brown sugar
3 teaspoons cinnamon

GLAZE:
½ cup powdered sugar
Milk (about 2–3 teaspoons)

For the dough: Preheat oven to 400°F. Spray 12 muffin cups with nonstick cooking spray. In a large bowl, combine flour, sugar, baking powder, and salt. Cut in butter until crumbly. Make a well in the center. Add milk; stir to form a soft dough. Turn out onto a floured surface. Knead 8-10 times. Roll dough into a ⅓-inch thick, 10x12-inch rectangle.

For the filling: Combine softened butter, brown sugar, and cinnamon; sprinkle onto dough. Roll up, jelly-roll style, starting from the long side. Seal the seam. Slice the roll into 12 pieces. Put pieces, cut-sides-down, into the muffin cups. Bake for 20–22 minutes. Remove from oven. Cool for 1 minute; turn out onto a wire rack. Cool slightly; drizzle with glaze. Serve warm or cold.

For the glaze: In a small bowl, add powdered sugar and stir in enough milk to reach a drizzling consistency.

Star of Texas

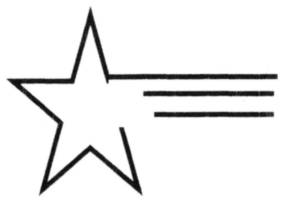

At this peaceful and secluded bed and breakfast just 4 miles from Brownwood, Texas, you will find yourself hidden on a tranquil hillside. Star of Texas is a wonderful alternative to hotel lodging. Here, you will experience the natural beauty and quiet serenity of central Texas. Stroll across its 25 acres, or relax under a vast Texas starlit sky.

Settle down to a blissful night's sleep and awaken to the singing of birds and a great hot country breakfast that is delivered to your cottage to be enjoyed in your room or on your private porch.

If you are a shopper there is a little gift shop next to the main house that offers many handcrafted items. Don, an artist Blacksmith, has an assortment of beautifully, crafted crosses and other forged items. Innkeeper, Debbie, works with clay and offers pottery pieces. Cookbooks, soaps, and other items too numerous to mention are for sale.

INNKEEPERS: Don and Debbie Morelock

ADDRESS: 650 Morelock Lane, Brownwood, Texas 76801

TELEPHONE: (325) 646-4128; (800) 850-2003

E-MAIL: relaxing@star-of-texas.com

WEBSITE: www.star-of-texas.com

ROOMS: 4 Cottages; 1 Suite; 1 Tipi; Private Baths

CHILDREN: Unable to accommodate

PETS: Call ahead; Resident pets

Cheddar Biscuits

Makes 4 Large Biscuits

"These hearty biscuits are a favorite – there is never a crumb left."
—INNKEEPER, *Star of Texas*

1 cup whole-wheat baking mix
   such as Hodgson Mill Insta-Bake mix)
$\frac{1}{3}$ cup milk
1 tablespoon fresh tarragon; chopped
   (or 1 teaspoon dried)
½ cup (2-ounces) cheddar cheese, grated
1½ tablespoons butter, melted
Garlic bread sprinkle (such as McCormick's)

Preheat oven to 425°F. Spray a baking sheet with nonstick cooking spray. In a small bowl, combine baking mix, milk, tarragon, and cheese. Form 4 biscuits by dropping dough, about 2 inches apart, onto the baking sheet. Bake for 20 minutes, or until the biscuits are golden brown.

While biscuits are baking, melt butter and garlic sprinkles together. Brush on tops of biscuits just before serving.

Good biscuits are
divinely inspired.
—ANONYMOUS

BROWN PELICAN INN

A BAYSIDE BED & BREAKFAST

The Brown Pelican Inn offers some of the finest accommodations in south Texas. Situated on the quiet bay shoreline of the famed South Padre Island, the inn boasts eight elegant guest rooms decorated with American and English antiques, and each has a private bath.

Several rooms have spectacular bay views, and the covered porch is a favorite vantage point from which to enjoy the sunset.

Texas' "best beach" is just a two-block stroll from your front door, and truly superb dining with the freshest seafood is only minutes away. Recreational options abound, and can keep even the most active well entertained. Try your hand at kite boarding or windsurfing. This is also a bird-watchers paradise—but that you can do from the comfort of your lawn chair!

INNKEEPERS: Chris and Yves de Diesbach
ADDRESS: 207 West Aries, South Padre Island, Texas 78597
MAILING: (PO Box 2667) 78597
TELEPHONE: (956) 761-2722
E-MAIL: innkeeper@brownpelican.com
WEBSITE: www.brownpelican.com
ROOMS: 8 Rooms; Private baths
CHILDREN: Age 12 and older welcome
PETS: Not allowed

Our Granola

Makes 6 to 8 Cups

3 cups old-fashioned rolled oats
1 cup sunflower seeds
1 cup white sesame seeds
1 cup applesauce
2 teaspoons ground cinnamon
1 teaspoon ground ginger
¾ cup brown rice syrup
3 tablespoons thin honey
½ cup light brown sugar
1 cup almonds
2 tablespoons sunflower oil
1 cup raisins or dried fruit of choice

Preheat oven to 350°F. In a large bowl, mix all ingredients except the raisins or dried fruit. Spread mixture on a large lightly greased baking tray; put in oven. Bake for 40 minutes; turning mixture every 10 minutes allowing granola to brown evenly. Cool granola completely; stirring occasionally to keep the granola from "clumping." Add fruit.

GEORGE BLUCHER HOUSE

High on the bluff overlooking Corpus Christi Bay, George Anton von Blucher and his bride built their galleried Victorian home in 1904. Now known as the George Blucher House, the inn exudes an understated elegance and the hospitality of bygone days. Nestled quietly beneath towering magnolia, elm, Anahuac, pecan and oak trees, this historic home sits just across the street from Blucher Park, an internationally renowned bird sanctuary. The inn is just a short stroll to unique downtown shops, upscale restaurants and a sparkling bay front and marina with colorful sailboats.

The innkeeper is a native of south Texas. The opening of the inn was a culmination of a 15-year dream come true. After staying in bed and breakfasts for many years throughout the States as well as Europe, Ms. Smith incorporated what she felt to be the best touches each of them had to offer.

INNKEEPER:	Tracey Love Smith
ADDRESS:	211 North Carrizo, Corpus Christi, Texas 78401
TELEPHONE:	(361) 884-4884; (866) 884-4884; (361) 884-4885 fax
E-MAIL:	blucherhousebnb@sbcglobal.net
WEBSITE:	www.georgeblucherhouse.com
ROOMS:	5 Rooms; 1 Suite; Private baths
CHILDREN:	Call ahead
PETS:	Not allowed; Resident dog & cat

George Blucher House Crunchy Granola

Makes 8 to 10 Cups

"Serve with plain or fruit yogurt, milk or cream. For a real treat, reserve coconut milk (if using fresh coconut slivers in the granola) and pour over the granola instead of the yogurt or milk."
—INNKEEPER, *George Blucher House*

4 cups old-fashioned rolled oats
   (not quick-cooking oats)
1 cup wheat germ
½ cup All-Bran Original cereal
2 (6-ounce) packages Planters trail mix
   (any variety without candy)
2–3 tablespoons sesame seeds
1 cup honey
1 cup canola oil
1 teaspoon cinnamon
1 (6-ounce) package dried Mariani Berries 'N Cherries
   (a blend of dried blueberries, strawberries, cherries
   and cranberries) or your choice of dried fruit
10–12 dried apricots, chopped
Fresh or dried coconut slivers (optional)

Preheat oven to 300°F. In a large bowl, combine oats, wheat germ, All-Bran, trail mix, and sesame seeds; set aside. In a small saucepan, heat together honey, oil, and cinnamon; stir until well mixed. Pour hot honey mixture over oat mixture; stir to combine. Spread evenly onto 2 large, greased baking sheets. Bake for 30–40 minutes, stirring every 10 minutes, until the mixture is toasted a light golden brown. Cool completely, stirring occasionally to keep the granola from "clumping."

When granola is cool, add Berries 'N Cherries, apricots and coconut; mix well. Store airtight in the refrigerator or freezer (if frozen, allow granola to come to room temperature before serving). This granola will keep for months.

Mansion at Judge's Hill

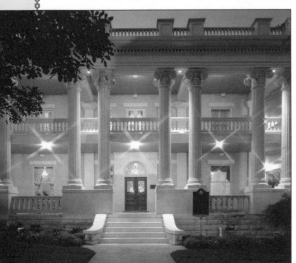

Built in 1900, the historic Goodall Wooten House is now home to Austin's premier boutique hotel and fine dining restaurant. The re-invention of this architectural masterpiece has created a plush haven where guests can retreat from the bustling streets of downtown Austin. The fine accommodations at the Mansion at Judges' Hill furnish all of the luxurious niceties necessary for a restful and carefree stay. The guest service staff is available twenty-four hours a day. Indulge in the in-room spa services. Take advantage of the business, laundry, and babysitting services. Complimentary parking, local newspapers, and day passes to a comprehensive local fitness facility are given to all overnight guests.

The elegant and refined Judges' Hill Restaurant offers an amazing culinary experience. Dine in the exquisite dining room, intimate lounge, or breezy veranda and delight in the seasonal menu blending fresh flavors from around the world. There are a plethora of choices on the ever-expanding wine list for a special libation to compliment your meal.

INNKEEPER: Lisa Wiedemann

ADDRESS: 1900 Rio Grande, Austin, Texas 78705

TELEPHONE: (512) 495-1800; (800) 311-1619; (512) 476-4769 fax

E-MAIL: lisa@judgeshill.com

WEBSITE: www.judgeshill.com

ROOMS: 48 Rooms; 2 Suites; Private Baths

CHILDREN: Welcome

PETS: Dogs and Cats welcome

Lisa's Award-Winning Granola

Makes 10 to 12 Cups

6 cups old-fashioned rolled oats
1 cup wheat germ
1 cup All-Bran cereal
1 cup nuts (of your choosing)
1 cup coconut
½ cup brown sugar
1 teaspoon cinnamon
1 cup honey
½ cup canola oil

Preheat oven to 300°F. In large mixing bowl, mix together first
5 ingredients. Add brown sugar and cinnamon; mix well. In a
small bowl, combine honey and oil; heat to slightly blend (about
45 seconds in the microwave). Pour honey and oil mixture over
the dry ingredients; mix well. Bake for 25–30 minutes; stirring
very 10 minutes.

Egg Entrées

Egg
Entrées

> "Love and eggs
> are best when
> they are fresh."
>
> — RUSSIAN PROVERB

BEAUREGARD HOUSE

The quiet elegance of the King William Historic District of downtown San Antonio is where you will find the Beauregard House Bed & Breakfast Inn. Enjoy the beauty of this historic district from one of the two porches available for your relaxation.

Just one block from the River Walk and within easy walking distance to the Alamo and Convention Center, the Beauregard House is the perfect place for business travelers and vacationers alike.

The individual rooms and suites are as uniquely furnished as their intriguing names suggest. The Mozart Room, the Picasso Room, the Firenze Room—and the Lady Di, Le Champagne, and Monaco Suites. You will have to return often to try them all.

INNKEEPERS: Kenneth Mohundro and Roland Quintanilla

ADDRESS: 215 Beauregard Street, San Antonio, Texas 78204

TELEPHONE: (210) 222-1198; (888) 667-0555

E-MAIL: relax@thebeauregardhouse.com

WEBSITE: www.beauregardhouse.com

ROOMS: 3 Rooms; 3 Suites; Private baths

CHILDREN: Age 16 and older welcome

PETS: Not allowed; Resident dog

Beauregard House River Breakfast

Makes 4 Servings

*"A delightful Southern breakfast of creamy eggs
and river trout. "Hot-smoked" salmon fillet (not "lox")
would be a delicious substitute for the trout, if desired."*
—INNKEEPER, *Beauregard House*

8 eggs
1 (1½-ounce) package smoked trout fillet,
   broken into ½-inch pieces
4 ounces cream cheese, room temperature,
   cut into ½-inch pieces
½ cup chopped green onions
1½ tablespoons chopped fresh dill
   (plus 4 sprigs for garnish)
Salt and pepper, to taste
2½ tablespoons butter

In a large bowl, beat eggs with a whisk. Add trout, cream cheese, green onions, chopped dill, salt and pepper; stir to mix.

In a large skillet, melt butter over medium heat. Add egg mixture; stir gently until eggs are set, but still moist, about 4 minutes. Divide eggs between 4 plates. Garnish each serving with a dill sprig.

1110 CARRIAGE HOUSE INN

The Carriage House Inn is close to historic downtown Austin and a short walk from the University of Texas. This two-story Colonial home is graced with many windows and accentuated by stately trees. An expansive deck, a pagoda gazebo, and a koi pond with a waterfall complete the idyllic setting. The interior of the inn features hardwood floors, antique tile, and a friendly ghost. Lava rock from a volcano in the area was used to build the guesthouse on the property. Fresh flowers adorn each room, each suite, and the cottages.

The full breakfast served at the Carriage House has been selected as one of the top ten best country breakfasts in the United States. Guests enjoy their own table as they savor the fresh, and often organic, morning meal. The menu changes daily and may include homemade waffles, scones, and biscuits.

INNKEEPERS:	Tressie Damron
ADDRESS:	1110 West 22½ Street, Austin, Texas 78705
TELEPHONE:	(512) 472-2333; (866) 472-2333; (512) 476-0218 fax
E-MAIL:	dcarriagehouse@aol.com
WEBSITE:	www.carriagehouseinn.org
ROOMS:	7 Rooms; 3 Suites; 2 Cottages; Private baths
CHILDREN:	Age 16 and older welcome
PETS:	Not allowed

Basil Breakfast Tacos

Makes 12 Tacos

*"I created this recipe because we love basil,
and our herb garden supplies me with lots of it."*
—INNKEEPER, *1110 Carriage House Inn*

6 eggs
½ cup Monterey Jack or
    Cream Havarti cheese, grated
or
1/4 cup Dutch Gouda Goat Cheese, grated
12 corn tortillas
⅓ cup basil pesto

In a small bowl, scramble eggs and cheese together. In a warm oven, slightly heat each tortilla. Spread 1 teaspoon of basil pesto on each warm tortilla; add egg and cheese mixture on each tortilla; roll and serve on plate with fresh fruit.

VARIATION:
If you want to add meat, lay a thin slice of turkey on the tortilla before the egg mixture.

Never work before breakfast;

if you have to work before breakfast,

eat your breakfast first.

—JOSH BILLINGS

OUTPOST AT CEDAR CREEK

Featured in the best-selling travel book, *1000 Places to See Before You Die,* this 1880s restored farmstead is a luxurious way to immerse yourself in some real Texas history. The historic log home of Gideon Lincecum, an early German pioneer and naturalist, still stands on the property.

Enjoy a lazy breakfast in the Ranger's Lounge and Conference Center and stroll through gardens filled with native plants. This 51 acre getaway in secluded Hill Country is one of the reasons why this is one of the great places to stay in Texas.

INNKEEPER: Lenore Prud'Homme

ADDRESS: 5808 Wagner Road, Round Top, Texas 78954

TELEPHONE: (979) 836-4975; (888) 433-5791; (979) 826-7577 fax

E-MAIL: stay@outpostinn.com

WEBSITE: www.outpostinn.com

ROOMS: 10 Rooms; 1 Suite; 3 Cottages; 11 Private baths, 2 shared

CHILDREN: Age 12 and older welcome

PETS: Not allowed; Resident dog and cats

Eggs Boudreaux

Makes 6 Servings

CRAWFISH POT:

1 box crawfish boil	1 clove garlic
1 lemon	3 pounds live crawfish or
2 teaspoons Tabasco sauce	¾ pounds of meat

EGGS:

8 ounces (1½ cup)	12 large Grade AA eggs
Monterey Jack cheese, grated	¾ cup milk
4 scallions, chopped,	Salt and pepper, to taste
including the green stalks	4 tablespoons butter

GARNISH:

Cilantro leaves, whole	Cooked, unpeeled, whole crawfish

For the Crawfish: In a large stockpot, bring 4 quarts of water to a boil; add the first 5 ingredients; cover and cook for 20 minutes. Drop the live crawfish in the boiling water. Boil 5-6 minutes, or until the shells become bright red and the crawfish float to the surface. Remove the pot from the stove; put on ice to stop the cooking. When cool, remove the crawfish; break open the tail and remove the meat. Reserve 6 whole crawfish for garnish. The tail meat may be covered and refrigerated for 2–3 days until ready to serve.

For the eggs: In a large bowl combine eggs and milk and beat well. Season with salt and pepper. In a frying pan, melt butter until it bubbles. When bubbling subsides, add egg mixture. As the bottom layers begin to set, gently scrap the pan with a spatula. Continue the slow, gentle scraping until the eggs look half done. For the last 30 seconds, add the cheese, scallions and 2 cups of the crawfish meat. Combine the ingredients by continuing to gently scrap the pan.

Place a mound of Eggs Boudreaux on warm plates. Garnish with a sprig of cilantro and cooked, unpeeled, whole crawfish. Serve immediately with toast or English muffins and fresh strawberries.

WOODBURN HOUSE

This elegant three-story home built in 1909 has been transformed into a beautiful bed and breakfast inn. It is located in Hyde Park, a National Register Historical District, just two miles from downtown Austin, and one mile from the University of Texas at Austin.

The house was named for Bettie Hamilton Woodburn and her husband, who bought the house in 1924. She was the daughter and speechwriter for Andrew Jackson Hamilton, a provisional governor of Texas, and a personal friend of Abraham Lincoln. Today the house is listed on the National Register of Historic Places and is designated a City of Austin Historical Landmark.

INNKEEPERS:	Kristen and Noel De La Rosa
ADDRESS:	4401 Avenue D, Austin, Texas 78751
TELEPHONE:	(512) 458-4335; (888) 690-9763
E-MAIL:	woodburnhouse-austin@hotmail.com
WEBSITE:	www.woodburnhouse.com
ROOMS:	6 Rooms; 1 Suite; 1 Cottage; 6 Private baths, 2 shared
CHILDREN:	Unable to accommodate
PETS:	Not allowed

Southwestern Rolled Omelet with
Chile Con Queso Filling and Pico de Gallo

Makes 5 to 6 Servings

OMELET:
1 cup milk
6 eggs

3 tablespoons butter, melted
$1/3$ cup all-purpose flour

PICO DE GALLO:
3 tablespoons lime juice
½ cup sweet onion, chopped
2 tablespoons fresh jalapeño,
   seeded, minced

½ teaspoon Kosher salt, or to taste
½ teaspoon freshly ground black
   black pepper, or to taste
2 tablespoons fresh cilantro, chopped

CHILI CON QUESO:
8 ounces Velvetta cheese,
   cut into 1-inch dice
1 cup cheddar cheese, shredded
½ cup heavy cream
1 small tomato, minced

½ small onion, minced
1 jalapeño, seeded, minced
Sour cream, to serve
Sliced avocado, to garnish

Preheat oven to 400°F. Spray a 9x13-inch baking dish (not a cooking sheet) with a vegetable spray. Line with parchment paper, (including the sides of the pan), and spray again to coat the parchment paper.

For the pico de gallo: In a small bowl, combine limejuice and onions; marinate for 15 minutes. Add the remaining ingredients; mix well; remove excess liquid before serving.

For the Omelet: In a large bowl, combine milk, eggs, butter and ½ of the pico de gallo. Beat until well blended and somewhat frothy. Pour mixture into the prepared baking pan. Bake for 10–15 minutes.

For the chile con queso: Combine cheeses in a double boiler or crock pot and melt at low heat. When cheese is melted, add the cream; stir until combined. Add remaining ingredients.

When the omelet is cooked, remove from the oven. Pour ¾ of the chili con queso on the eggs; spread evenly. Starting with the shorter end, roll the egg into an omelet by using one hand to pull the parchment paper. With the other hand, use a large spatula to keep the eggs from sliding. Carefully lift the omelet onto a plate. Sprinkle with more chili con queso and the remaining pico de gallo. Slice the omelet into 5 pieces and serve. Dollops of sour cream or sliced avocado may be added as garnish.

MARIPOSA RANCH

Mariposa Ranch Bed & Breakfast is located on a 100-acre working ranch along the historic La Bahia Trail. Accommodations include an 1870 plantation home, an 1820 log cabin, a quaint cottage, an 1836 Greek revival home, a turn-of-the-century Texas farmhouse (the original homestead on this working ranch), a ranch hand's bunkhouse, a cozy settler's cottage and a real cowboy cabin.

Maiposa offers one-stop shopping for your wedding. Let Mariposa be "yours" from Friday until Sunday and enjoy all of your festivities here, from the rehearsal dinner to the wedding and reception, and a beautiful buffet breakfast the morning after.

"A romantic and historic getaway
with warm hospitality and country elegance."
—*Southern Living* MAGAZINE

INNKEEPERS:	Johnna and Charles Chamberlain
ADDRESS:	8904 Mariposa Lane, Brenham, Texas 77833
TELEPHONE:	(979) 836-4737; (877) 647-4774; (979) 836-2565 fax
E-MAIL:	info@mariposaranch.com
WEBSITE:	www.mariposaranch.com
ROOMS:	4 Rooms; 2 Suites; 5 Cottages; Private baths
CHILDREN:	Welcome
PETS:	Not allowed; Resident cat & dogs

Texas Oven Omelet

Makes 12 Servings

"A breakfast entrée that tastes great and is very colorful to serve. The omelet can be prepared the night before and baked in the morning."
—INNKEEPER, *Mariposa Ranch*

12 eggs
1 cup sour cream
2 green bell peppers, diced
1 (8-ounce) carton sliced fresh mushrooms
1 (15-ounce) can diced tomatoes, drained
1 (16-ounce) box Velveeta cheese, cubed
1 pound ham, chopped
½ stick (¼ cup) butter, cut into small pieces

Preheat oven to 325°F. Butter a 9x13-inch baking dish. In a large bowl, beat eggs and sour cream. Stir in the remaining ingredients; mix well. Pour mixture into baking dish. (At this point, the dish may be covered and refrigerated overnight.)

Bake for 60 minutes (an additional 10–15 minutes of baking time will be needed if the mixture was refrigerated overnight.) Let stand for 10 minutes before serving.

OMELET—the word comes from the French "lamelle" (thin strip) because of its flat shape. It was originally known as alumelle, then alumette, and finally amelette.

CHASKA HOUSE

Waxahachie is located in the north Texas prairies and lakes region thirty minutes south of Dallas. Just a short stroll from historic Waxahachie's town square, Chaska House Lodging Properties provide premier bed and breakfast accommodations, guest cottages, corporate lodging, and a classic wedding and reception site on three historic properties.

Built in 1900, The Chaska House Bed & Breakfast is a two-story frame home with twenty-one Ionic columns. This recently renovated National Register-listed home offers guestrooms and suites reflecting the lifestyles and works of well-known authors including Samuel Clemens, F. Scott Fitzgerald, Margaret Mitchell, and William Shakespeare. Ernest Hemingway is personified a few steps away in Hemingway's Retreat. Overlooking a lush tropical courtyard, two private cottages have been designed in the style of Hemingway's Key West home.

A full southern breakfast is available for bed and breakfast and cottage guests at the Chaska House.

INNKEEPERS:	Louis and Linda Brown
ADDRESS:	716 West Main Street, Waxahachie, Texas 75165
TELEPHONE:	(972) 937-3390; (800) 931-3390; (972) 937-1780 fax
E-MAIL:	chaskabb@sbcglobal.net
WEBSITE:	www.chaskabb.com
ROOMS:	5 Rooms; 2 Cottages; Private baths
CHILDREN:	Age 12 and older are welcome
PETS:	Not allowed

Eggs Benedict (Arnold)

Makes 12 Servings

"Not the real thing, but 'Traitorously' good!
Plates always return to the kitchen clean."
—Innkeeper, *The Chaska House*

16 eggs, hard-boiled, peeled and
     sliced in egg slicer, $\frac{1}{8}$-inch
1 stick butter
1 cup flour
4 cups milk
10 ounces Cheese Whiz (or grated, aged cheddar)
10 ounces sour cream
1¾ pounds bulk sausage
     (Jimmy Dean Hot), lightly fried,
     crumbled, drained
Salt and pepper, to taste
12 English muffins, divided and toasted
Sprig of parsley, mint, or fruit, to garnish

Preheat oven to 325°F. Spray a 3 quart, 9x13-inch casserole dish with nonstick vegetable spray. Layer with egg slices. In a large saucepan, melt butter; slowly add flour until butter is absorbed. Add milk and stir constantly over medium heat until mixture is slightly thickened. Stir in Cheese Whiz and sour cream. Season, to taste.

Pour mixture evenly over egg slices; top with sausage; cover with aluminum foil. Bake for 25 minutes. Remove foil and bake for an additional 10 minutes until sausage is brown and eggs are bubbly.

Serve on toasted English muffins. Sprinkle with paprika and garnish with a piece of fruit, sprig of mint or parsley.

DECKER CREEK
BED & BREAKFAST & BISCUIT

"Our full name is Decker Creek Bed and Breakfast and Biscuit.
At Decker Creek, dogs are guests, too."
—INNKEEPERS, Decker Creek B&B&B

The Decker Creek cabin is just fifteen miles from Austin and was built in 2006 with dog guests in mind. There are wooden and tile floors, a fenced yard, screened porch, plus an outdoor dog wash area. Dog food bowls, dog sheets, blankets, and beds are provided inside the cabin. Homemade dog biscuits are prepared for the canine guests.

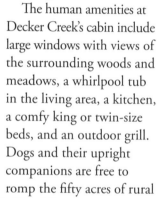

The human amenities at Decker Creek's cabin include large windows with views of the surrounding woods and meadows, a whirlpool tub in the living area, a kitchen, a comfy king or twin-size beds, and an outdoor grill. Dogs and their upright companions are free to romp the fifty acres of rural countryside intersected by Decker Creek. The full country breakfast is served, by prior arrangement, at a time that is convenient for the human guests. The huevos rancheros are made with farm-fresh eggs and the coffee is fabulous.

INNKEEPERS:	Pat and Byron Rathbun
ADDRESS:	16029 Decker Lake Road, Manor, Texas 78653
TELEPHONE:	(512) 743-8835; (512) 743-8090
E-MAIL:	pat.rathburn@gmail.com
WEBSITE:	www.deckercreek.com
ROOMS:	1 Cottage; Private bath
CHILDREN:	Welcome, if well behaved
PETS:	Dogs are welcome; Resident dogs

STUFFED POBLANOS

Makes 2 Servings

"I have served this to guests who don't want the usual sweet breakfasts—they have all loved it. Poblanos can vary in heat, so make sure guests know that this dish can be spicy."
—INNKEEPER, *Decker Creek*

Oil for frying, 2–3 cups
2 poblano peppers
1 cup Mexican chorizo
4 eggs, beaten
1 cup queso fresco
    (a white, slightly salty Mexican cheese;
    similar to feta or farmer's cheese), crumbled
2 green onions, chopped
    with some of the green stalks
1 cup Mexican cheese, shredded
½ cup salsa

In a large frying pan, fry whole peppers in hot oil until blistered on all sides. Remove peppers from the oil; blot dry; place in a paper sack to steam for 10 minutes.

In a frying pan, crumble the chorizo and cook until done. Drain the chorizo on paper towels. Swab out the frying pan; put eggs in pan and scramble until almost done. Stir in queso fresco and green onions. Cook until blended.

Pull the skins off the peppers, make a slit in each one and pull out the seeds and membranes. Stuff the egg and sausage mixture in the peppers; place on a baking sheet and top with shredded cheese. Place under a broiler for a minute or two until cheese is melted.

Place about ¼ cup of salsa on each plate; top with the pepper.

TIP:
You can fry corn tortilla wedges in the oil before frying the peppers. These can be served on the side.

MUNZESHEIMER MANOR

Munzesheimer Manor is a magnificent testimony to the Victorian era, built at the turn of the century by a German immigrant for his new bride. The house features large rooms with high ceilings, seven fireplaces with antique mantles, many bay windows, and a large wrap-around porch complete with rocking chairs and wicker furniture.

Weddings at Munzesheimer Manor are very intimate and beautiful (a maximum of 50 guests can be accommodated). A bride descending the staircase at the end of the reception hall and meeting the wedding party in front of the antique mantle in the adjacent parlor is truly a picture to behold. The "standing parlor weddings" are very unique and create lasting memories for the bride and groom and the guests. Immediate family members are seated—the guests remain standing.

"One of the 12 best bed and breakfasts in Texas."
—THE DALLAS MORNING NEWS

INNKEEPERS:	Bob and Sherry Murray
ADDRESS:	202 North Newsom, Mineola, Texas 75773
TELEPHONE:	(903) 569-6634; (888) 569-6634; (903) 569-9940 fax
E-MAIL:	innkeeper@munzesheimer.com
WEBSITE:	www.munzesheimer.com
ROOMS:	4 Rooms; 3 Cottages; Private baths
CHILDREN:	Welcome; Call ahead
PETS:	Not allowed; Resident dog

Chile Cheese Puff

Makes 8 Servings

*"This is a 'real' Texas breakfast served with
biscuits and gravy and lots of hot coffee."*
—INNKEEPER, *Munzesheimer Manor*

2 (4-ounce) cans green chilies, drained, chopped
4 cups (16 ounces) grated cheddar/Jack cheese
14 large eggs
2 cups milk
¼ cup baking mix (such as Bisquick)
Salsa, for serving
Sour cream, for serving

Preheat oven to 350°F. Spread chilies in an ungreased 9x13-inch
baking dish. Cover chilies with cheese. In a large bowl, whisk
together eggs, milk, and baking mix; pour over cheese. Bake for
40–45 minutes. Cut into squares and serve with salsa and sour cream.

*The egg is to cuisine
what the article is to speech.*

— ANONYMOUS

The Full Moon Inn

The Full Moon Inn is an historic 1860 property nestled on 12 manicured acres with six enchanting rooms rich with charm and class. The inn is a scenic one-hour drive from San Antonio or Austin, and just minutes from three wineries, two state parks, the Guadalupe River, the historic Luckenbach Dance Hall and great antiquing in Fredericksburg.

The Old Smokehouse Cottage, decorated with sunflowers, picket fence, barn wood and cozy comfort, was featured in Southern Living's Texas Vacations.

The Full Moon Inn is unique in that it welcomes pets—with a few rules! Please call ahead to discuss your pet and be aware that there will be an extra charge.

"Thanks for the wonderful time. The accommodations ...
were fantastic with lots of room for our three-month old son
and the two dogs!" —Guest

INNKEEPER: Captain Matthew Carinhas

ADDRESS: 3234 Luckenbach Road, Fredericksburg, Texas 78624

TELEPHONE: (830) 997-2205; (800) 997-1124; (830) 997-1115 fax

E-MAIL: info@fullmooninn.com

WEBSITE: www.fullmooninn.com

ROOMS: 6 Rooms; Private baths

CHILDREN: Welcome

PETS: Call ahead; Welcome with a few rules; Resident pets

Eggs Luckenbach

Makes 6 to 8 Servings

"We like to serve Eggs Luckenbach with French toast and German sausage. The eggs hold well on the stove top or in a warm oven while finishing up last-minute breakfast preparations."
—INNKEEPER, *The Full Moon Inn*

3 tablespoons bacon drippings
   (for the best flavor), or butter or canola oil
1 cup French's French fried onions
½ cup green onions, chopped
12 eggs
2 tablespoons Louisiana hot sauce
Suggested garnishes: mint leaves,
   strawberries or chopped green onion tops

Heat bacon drippings. In a 10-inch nonstick pan, heat bacon drippings over medium heat. Add French fried onions and green onions; cook just until hot. In a blender, mix eggs and hot sauce on low speed (or beat thoroughly with a hand mixer); add to hot mixture in pan. Lower heat and scramble eggs until almost done, but still moist.

Using a wooden spatula, pat the eggs down until the mixture is smooth in the pan. Cover with a lid or foil. Turn off the heat and let stand on the burner or put the pan in a preheated 185°F oven for 5-6 minutes. Remove from heat; cut into wedges to serve. Garnish as desired.

PANIOLO RANCH

The Paniolo Ranch B&B Spa is a romantic resort retreat located in the Heart of the Texas Hill Country and just a stone's throw from historic Boerne, Texas. This spa offers outstanding recreation and relaxation, whether for a honeymoon, anniversary, birthday, or just a simple "getaway weekend." Enjoy breakfast on your private patio or have a cup of coffee by the pool before diving in for a refreshing swim to start your day.

There is so much to do at Paniolo you will need your evenings to relax. There are picnics at the lake, fossil hunting in the spring, gardening in the greenhouse, dabbling in the Art Studio, jewelry making, and picking fruit in the orchards.

The cottages are more appropriately named "houses" and there is a definite Hawaiian flavor in the ambiance.

"The Paniolo Ranch B&B Spa marries Hawaiian luxuries and Lone Star traditions for a Texas ranch getaway like none other."
—*TEXAS HIGHWAY'S* MAGAZINE

INNKEEPER: Judy Kennell
ADDRESS: 1510 FM 473, Boerne, Texas 78006
TELEPHONE: (830) 324-6665; (866) 726-4656; (830) 324-6665 fax
E-MAIL: paniolo@panioloranch.com
WEBSITE: www.panioloranch.com
ROOMS: 4 Cottages; Private baths
CHILDREN: Age 16 and older are welcome
PETS: Not allowed; Resident dogs, horses, donkeys, chickens, and llama

Paniolo Olé Breakfast Casserole

Makes 8 Servings

1 pound pork sausage

12 eggs

2 7-ounce bottles of green chile sauce

1 teaspoon dry mustard

1 tablespoon Worcestershire sauce

1 teaspoon onion salt

Black pepper, to taste

½ cup green onions, chopped

1 pound mild cheddar cheese, grated

1 pound sharp cheddar cheese, grated

2 cups hash brown potatoes, uncooked

Preheat oven to 350°F. Grease a 9x13-inch baking pan. In a frying pan, brown sausage; drain grease; set aside. In a blender, combine eggs, green chile sauce, dry mustard, Worcestershire sauce, onion salt, and pepper; mix well. In a large bowl, combine egg mixture, sausage, onions, cheeses, and hash browns. Combine well; pour into baking pan.

Bake for 35–45 minutes or until set.

Serve with peach or pineapple salsa; or with black beans and tortillas for a breakfast burrito.

A BECKMANN INN AND CARRIAGE HOUSE

The gourmet breakfast at A Beckmann Inn is served in the formal dining room with china, crystal, and silver. The morning menu includes fresh ground coffee, specialty teas, uniquely blended fruit juices, an entrée, fresh fruit and coffee cake, muffins or pastries.

Be sure to save room for A Beckmann Inn's signature second course "breakfast dessert."

The Carriage House lodging is adjacent to the main house and was built around the turn of the century. It has been completely renovated, featuring shuttered windows with flower-filled window boxes, gardens, balcony and patio areas, and has two rooms for guest accommodations.

INNKEEPER:	Charles Stallcup
ADDRESS:	222 East Guenther Street, San Antonio, Texas 78204
TELEPHONE:	(210) 229-1449; (800) 945-1449
E-MAIL:	stay@beckmanninn.com
WEBSITE:	www.beckmanninn.com
ROOMS:	5 Rooms; Private baths
CHILDREN:	Age 12 and older welcome
PETS:	Not allowed

Southern Cornbread and Egg Casserole

Makes 12 Servings

*For a vegetarian casserole,
substitute diced green pepper and onion for the ham.*

1 cup yellow cornmeal
1 cup flour
¼ teaspoon baking soda
2 tablespoons sugar
1¼ cups buttermilk
1 egg plus 8 eggs
¾ cup diced cooked ham
1½ cups (6 ounces) cheddar or Swiss cheese
2 cups milk
Dash of Pickapeppa or Worcestershire sauce
Salt and pepper, to taste

Preheat oven to 375°F. Spray a 9-inch round baking pan with nonstick cooking spray. In a large bowl, combine cornmeal, flour, baking soda, sugar, buttermilk, and 1 egg; stir just until combined. Pour into baking pan and bake for 25 minutes, or until a toothpick inserted in the center comes out clean. Allow cornbread to cool.

When the cornbread is cooled, crumble it into large chunks; put it in a 9x13-inch baking pan sprayed with nonstick cooking spray. Sprinkle the ham and cheese over the top.

In a large bowl, whisk together 8 eggs, milk, Pickapeppa sauce, and salt and pepper. Pour evenly over the ingredients in the baking pan. Bake for 30 minutes, or until done. Let stand for 5 minutes before serving.

CAMP DAVID

Camp David Bed & Breakfast offers the privacy of your own cottage along with a full gourmet breakfast brought to your door each morning. The cottages and Pecan Suite (in the main house) have English Country décor and are furnished with European and American antiques.

Most cottages have fully equipped kitchens, extra-large whirlpool tubs and gas log fireplaces. Front porches lined with rockers and bistro tables invite you to relax and enjoy the breezes from the pecan tree-shaded courtyard.

"It was my first visit to Fredericksburg, Texas and your inn was the best choice of all."

—GUEST

INNKEEPERS:	Molly and Bob Sagebiel
ADDRESS:	708 West Main, Fredericksburg, Texas 78624
TELEPHONE:	(830) 997-7797; (866) 427-8374
E-MAIL:	campdavidbb@austin.rr.com
WEBSITE:	www.campdavidbb.com
ROOMS:	1 Suite; 5 Cottages; Private baths
CHILDREN:	Age 12 and older welcome
PETS:	Not allowed

Eggs Amanda

Makes 2 Servings

*"Amanda is our younger daughter. Like many young women,
she doesn't always eat a big breakfast. But the first time I served this,
she almost ate the plate! It was her recommendation
to add the bacon ... a delicious suggestion!"*
—INNKEEPER, *Camp David*

ROLLS:
2 bolillo rolls (found in Mexican bakeries),
   or substitute crusty French bread sub rolls, unsliced
2 hard-boiled eggs, peeled and sliced
1½ cups white sauce (recipe follows)
Paprika, to garnish
Chives, chopped (or substitute chopped green onions)
2–4 tablespoons bacon, cooked, chopped

Preheat oven to 350°F. Lightly grease or spray the bottoms of
2 individual oval, shallow gratin dishes. Slice a thin layer off the
top of the rolls and remove the soft bread inside, leaving a "bread
shell." Lay the slices of egg inside the shell, using 1 egg per roll.

Ladle 1–2 tablespoons of white sauce into each dish. Place stuffed
roll on the sauce and ladle more sauce over the egg and roll. Sprinkle
with paprika and chives. Top with chopped bacon. Bake for 30 minutes. Serve hot.

WHITE SAUCE:
2 tablespoons butter
2 tablespoons flour
1½ cups whole milk or half & half
½ teaspoon cumin
Salt and pepper, to taste

In a medium saucepan, melt butter over low heat. Stir in flour;
cook until bubbly, stirring occasionally. Remove from heat. Slowly
whisk in the milk. Return to the stove and cook over low heat,
stirring constantly until thickened. Stir in cumin, salt and pepper.

PRINCE SOLMS INN

Prince Solms Inn opened its doors in 1898, and has been in continuous operation ever since, making it the oldest continuously operating inn/bed and breakfast in Texas. The Uptown Piano Bar in the cellar of the inn has been named "the most romantic spot in Texas" by *Ultra* magazine. The Bath Haus Spa in the carriage house offers a wide range of massage therapy services.

Or you are invited to sit back in one of the Adirondack chairs on the balcony and enjoy a cool evening breeze, or relax in a swing on the porch, and watch the sunset.

One of the more unusual remodeled accommodations at Prince Solms Inn began as a Feed Store and Stable around 1860. Adjacent to the inn, it originally served not only as a store, but as a place where business deals might be discussed while sitting around the large woodburning heater. One can imagine that the Civil War was one of the main topics of conversation in those early days.

INNKEEPER: Al Buttross

ADDRESS: 295 East San Antonio Street, New Braunfels, Texas 78130

TELEPHONE: (830) 625-9169; (800) 625-9169; (830) 625-2220 fax

E-MAIL: princesolmsinn@msn.com

WEBSITE: www.princesolmsinn.com

ROOMS: 8 Rooms; 5 Suites; 1 Cottage; Private baths

CHILDREN: Welcome in select portions of the Inn

PETS: Not allowed

Sunrise Eggs

Makes 1 Serving

1 egg
1 teaspoon heavy cream
salt and pepper, to taste
sprinkle of fresh basil, chopped
sprinkle of fresh thyme leaves
sprinkle of cheddar cheese, grated
sprinkle of parmesan cheese, grated
sprinkle of paprika
fresh parsley, to garnish

Preheat oven to 375°F. Spray large individual muffin cups with non-stick spray. Line each muffin cup with a foil muffin cup. Spray once again with non-stick spray. Break open egg into muffin cup. Add cream, salt, pepper, basil, and thyme. Cover egg with cheddar cheese. Add Parmesan cheese. Bake for 15 minutes, until yolk is hard. Turn out on to a plate and sprinkle with paprika and garnish with sprig of parsley.

I did toy with the idea

of doing a cookbook . . . I think

a lot of people who hate literature

but love fried eggs would buy it

if the price was right.

— GROUCHO MARX

BRAVA HOUSE

Located in the wonderful neighborhood of Old West Austin, Brava House provides a memorable stay in the Capitol City. It is one of Austin's first Victorian homes built in the late 1880s. The structure has been lovingly restored and features elegant antique furnishings and charming architectural details.

Enjoy the quiet, peaceful setting and private rooms, and still be within strolling distance of the shops, restaurants, art galleries, parks and nightlife in downtown Austin.

The Brava House is located just minutes from 6th Street, the Texas State Capitol, the University of Texas, the convention center, the Texas State History Museum, Barton Springs and the LBJ Library.

INNKEEPER:	Robin Kyle
ADDRESS:	1108 Blanco Street, Austin, Texas 78703
TELEPHONE:	(512) 478-5034 phone and fax
E-MAIL:	robin@bravahouse.com
WEBSITE:	www.bravahouse.com
ROOMS:	2 Rooms, 2 Suites; Private baths
CHILDREN:	Call ahead
PETS:	Call ahead; Resident dog

Egg Cups with Sun-Dried Tomatoes

Makes 6 Servings

"These are always a big hit with our guests!"
—INNKEEPER, *Brava House*

6 eggs
1 cup whole milk
1 teaspoon fresh basil, finely chopped
Salt and pepper, to taste (about a pinch each)
6 tablespoons sun-dried tomatoes, chopped,
    (drained, if oil-packed)
6 tablespoons feta cheese, crumbled

Preheat oven to 350°F. Spray 6 ramekins or deep custard cups (6-ounce capacity) with nonstick cooking spray. In a medium bowl, whisk together eggs, milk, basil, salt and pepper. Put 1 tablespoon sun-dried tomatoes and 1 tablespoon feta cheese into each ramekin. Divide the egg mixture between the ramekins (about ⅓ cup each).

Bake for about 30 minutes, or until puffed and a toothpick inserted in the center comes out clean.

Mansion at Judge's Hill

Built in 1900, the historic Goodall Wooten House is now home to Austin's premier boutique hotel and fine dining restaurant. The re-invention of this architectural masterpiece has created a plush haven where guests can retreat from the bustling streets of downtown Austin. The fine accommodations at the Mansion at Judges' Hill furnish all of the luxurious niceties necessary for a restful and carefree stay. The guest service staff is available twenty-four hours a day. Indulge in the in-room spa services. Take advantage of the business, laundry, and babysitting services. Complimentary parking, local newspapers, and day passes to a comprehensive local fitness facility are given to all overnight guests.

The elegant and refined Judges' Hill Restaurant offers an amazing culinary experience. Dine in the exquisite dining room, intimate lounge, or breezy veranda and delight in the seasonal menu blending fresh flavors from around the world. There are a plethora of choices on the ever-expanding wine list for a special libation to compliment your meal.

INNKEEPER: Lisa Wiedemann

ADDRESS: 1900 Rio Grande, Austin, Texas 78705

TELEPHONE: (512) 495-1800; (800) 311-1619; (512) 476-4769 fax

E-MAIL: lisa@judgeshill.com

WEBSITE: www.judgeshill.com

ROOMS: 48 Rooms; 2 Suites; Private Baths

CHILDREN: Welcome

PETS: Dogs and Cats welcome

Lisa's Baked Havarti Eggs

Makes 4 Servings

*"The National Egg Board recognized my recipe as original and easy.
We were featured in the National Egg Board brochure for 3 years."*
—INNKEEPER, *Mansion at Judges' Hill*

4 teaspoons butter

4 tablespoons half-and-half

4 large eggs

Salt and freshly ground pepper, to taste

4 heaping tablespoons Havarti cheese
   (do not substitute)

½ teaspoon dill

Preheat oven to 450°F. Place 1 teaspoon butter into each of the ramekin dishes; place in oven to melt butter. Remove from oven; add 1 tablespoon half-and-half; crack 1 egg into each ramekin. Season with salt and pepper. Cover each egg with 1 tablespoon Havarti. Sprinkle evenly with dill. Bake for 8–10 minutes, or until egg white is done with yolk softly cooked.

LittleGoose LakeHaus

Pause to appreciate the whimsical, pink concrete couch at the entrance to the private front yard of the LittleGoose LakeHaus. Continue toward the inn through the natural landscaping of the private front yard, up the little hill, and through the gate of the wooden picket fence and you will find this eclectic, original, small, and cozy bed and breakfast. The inn is perched on the south side of Canyon Lake near the Texas Hill Country town of Startzville. There is ample parking for guests, even if you bring a boat.

Lodge in a romantic mini-suite that includes the Gander Room with a dreamy, warm fireplace corner and a king-size bed with an artistic headboard fashioned out of copper pipe and intertwining vines. There is a secluded hot tub just outside of the Gander Room. The adjoining Breakfast Room has a lovely stained-glass window and a view of the yard and lake. A deck extends this room into the out-of-doors.

Comal Park is just down the hill and around the corner from LittleGoose Lakehaus. A nice swimming area and an offshore island are yours to explore in the park.

INNKEEPER: Sherry Gansle

ADDRESS: 1100 Hillcrest Forest, Canyon Lake, Texas 78133

TELEPHONE: (830) 899-3828; (866) 834-8160; (830) 899-5580 fax

E-MAIL: desk@littlegooselakehaus.com

WEBSITE: www.littlegooselakehaus.com

ROOMS: 1 Suite; Private bath

CHILDREN: Welcome

PETS: Not allowed

Herb-Baked Eggs

Makes 4 Servings

"Our guests rave about this dish.
Serving it in fanciful ramekins enhances the enjoyment."
—INNKEEPER, *LittleGoose Lakehaus*

4 thin slices ham
3 large eggs
1 teaspoon prepared mustard
¼ cup plain yogurt or sour cream
   (We prefer sour cream.)
¾ cup (3-ounces) Cheddar cheese,
   shredded, divided
2 teaspoons fresh chives, chopped
2 teaspoons fresh parsley, chopped
Springs of herbs to garnish

Preheat oven to 375°F. Grease four ramekins; line them with ham slices. In a medium bowl, beat eggs, mustard, and yogurt or sour cream. Stir ¼ cup of cheese into the egg mixture. In a small bowl, mix chives, parsley; add ½ of it to the egg mixture. Stir well; spoon into prepared ramekins. Sprinkle with remaining cheese and herbs.

Bake for 25–30 minutes until golden and set. Garnish with sprigs of herbs and serve in the ramekins—warning guests that they are hot.

Buttered toast goes well with this dish. For a heartier breakfast, we will often make this into 2 servings instead of four. You will need larger ramekins for this.

GARDEN MANOR
"Where Dallas and Fort Worth Meet"

A sweeping veranda overlooks the tranquil grounds of the Garden Manor located in Grapevine, one of the oldest towns in Texas. Over seventy shops in Grapevine's historic shopping district are within walking distance of the inn. With the Dallas–Fort Worth Airport only seven miles from Grapevine, Garden Manor Bed and Breakfast is a convenient resting place for the business traveler or visitor.

The décor in each guest room reflects the lovely outdoor garden. Every room has a private bath with European heated towel racks, garden-scented bath products, and two spa robes. Turndown service includes a box of fresh chocolate truffles. Early morning beverage service is provided and a full-course breakfast is served in the dining room.

The new garden room addition to the Manor has two sets of French doors that open onto the back and side lawns; a combination of indoor and outdoor space designed to accommodate events.

INNKEEPERS: Judy and Gunther Dusek

ADDRESS: 205 East College Street, Grapevine, Texas 76051

TELEPHONE: (817) 424-9177; (877) 424-9177

E-MAIL: info@gardenmanorbandb.com

WEBSITE: www.gardenmanorbandb.com

ROOMS: 3 Rooms; 1 Suite; Private baths

CHILDREN: Ages 12 and older are welcome

PETS: Not Allowed; Resident dog

Buttermilk Quiche

Makes 8 Servings

*"This dish is very flexible. It is delicious
with either bacon or ham, or eliminate meat for vegetarians
and substitute with sautéed onions and mushrooms.
Male guests often comment that this is a manly quiche!"*
—INNKEEPER, *Garden Manor*

1 refrigerated piecrust, 9-inch
8 slices thick-style bacon
12 eggs
1 cup buttermilk
4 green onions, thinly sliced
¾ cup Monterey Jack or cheddar cheese, shredded

Preheat oven to 375°F. Quiche may be made with a homemade piecrust, but the prepared refrigerated crust is very good and easy to use. Allow the refrigerated crust to soften at room temperature for 15 minutes. Press crust into a 9-inch pie plate according to the directions on the box.

In a skillet or in the oven, brown the bacon until cooked but not crisp. Set bacon aside on paper towels to cool and drain; cut into small pieces.

In a large bowl, beat eggs; add buttermilk; fold in green onions, cheese, and bacon pieces. Pour mixture into piecrust. Bake for 35–45 minutes. Remove from oven and allow quiche to set for 5 minutes. Serve with warm croissants and fresh fruit.

THE COLUMNS ON ALAMO

Your hosts, Art and Ellenor Link, invite you to relax and experience the charm of the Historic King William neighborhood with its many lovely old homes, while you stay in an elegant 1892 Greek revival mansion and 1901 guesthouse with spacious gardens. Surround yourself with the inn's antique furnishings, chandeliers, oriental rugs and stained glass.

Sleep in luxurious queen or king beds and pamper yourself with a full gourmet breakfast every day. Take your time—your resident hosts will help you plan a full day of sights and events unique to San Antonio. They can show you where to find off-the-beaten-path places and direct you to the best restaurants.

Enjoy the River Walk and The Alamo, great shopping and fine dining, bike or hike the Mission Trail, try the many premier golf courses.

The Rockhouse Cottage is a small, 1881 style limestone house set back among the trees. The décor celebrates the Texas cowboy heritage with comfortable rustic pine furniture and historic photos of cowboys at work and play.

INNKEEPERS: Ellenor and Art Link

ADDRESS: 1037 South Alamo, San Antonio, Texas 78210

TELEPHONE: (210) 271-3245; (800) 233-3364

E-MAIL: artlink@columnssanantonio.com

WEBSITE: www.columnssanantonio.com

ROOMS: 13 Rooms; 1 Cottage; Private baths

CHILDREN: Welcome

PETS: Not allowed

Texas Quiche

Makes 6 Servings

*"Green chilies, Tabasco sauce, black pepper and salsa
add a kick to this dish. A quiche designed for 'real men.'"*
—INNKEEPER, *The Columns on Alamo*

1 (9-inch) deep-dish piecrust, unbaked
   (thawed, if frozen)
1½ cups (6 ounces) Colby or
   Monterey Jack cheese, grated
1 (7 ounce) can green chilies,
   drained, chopped
3 eggs
1½ cups heavy cream
3 dashes Tabasco sauce
Black pepper, to taste
Red or green salsa, for serving

Preheat oven to 350°F. Layer the cheese, then the chilies into
the bottom of the crust. Beat together eggs, cream, Tabasco and
pepper. Pour the egg mixture over the cheese and chilies—do not
stir! Bake for 35–40 minutes, or until browned and a toothpick
inserted in center comes out clean. Serve hot, with salsa on the side.

MEMORY LANE

Enjoy your stay at Memory Lane while relaxing at the pool, taking a peaceful walk through the wildflower gardens, or enjoying a starlit night far from the lights of the city.

Located on 18 acres of rolling hillside, Memory Lane can easily accommodate group events such as weddings and corporate meetings.

If you are looking for an intimate, romantic weekend getaway, the Texas Suite is a perfect match. For longer stays try the Hill Country View Suite. Both suites have private entrances and offer a clean, healthy atmosphere with non-smoking, chemical free rooms.

INNKEEPER: Janet Morgan

ADDRESS: 403 K.C. Memory Lane, Dripping Springs, Texas 78620

MAILING: (PO Box 803) 78620

TELEPHONE: (512) 894-0700; (512) 905-2787

E-MAIL: janetmorgan@hughes.net

WEBSITE: www.memorylanebedandbreakfast.com

ROOMS: 2 Suites; Private baths

CHILDREN: Welcome

PETS: Not Allowed; Resident goats, chickens, donkey, horse, and cats

Summer
Tomato Basil Quiche

Makes 6 Servings

*"Guests enjoy the lovely garden and appreciate
the fresh tomatoes and basil that we harvest
just for their breakfast. Our chickens add to the
deliciously fresh flavor with their free range eggs."*
—Innkeeper, *Memory Lane*

1 refrigerated piecrust, 9-inch
    (prepared or homemade)
3 eggs, beaten
$\frac{1}{8}$ cup heavy cream
¼ cup feta cheese, crumbled
1 basil leaf, chopped
Salt and pepper, to taste
1 large tomato, thinly sliced, seeds removed

Preheat oven to 375°F. Roll out pie crust and put in pie plate or
quiche dish. In a small bowl, mix eggs, cream, feta cheese, basil,
salt and pepper. Pour ½ egg mixture into pie- crust. Lay ½ of the
tomato slices on top of egg mixture; pour remaining egg mixture
into piecrust; top with remaining tomato slices. Bake for 10 minutes.
reduce heat to 350°F; continue baking for an additional 20 minutes.

FAIR BREEZE COTTAGE

Fair Breeze Cottage is located on Old Spanish Bluff Road, bordering Bonaldo Creek in Historic Nacogdoches County. Rustic in nature, the cottage is surrounded by walnut trees and overlooks 46 pastoral acres. The quiet setting offers a peaceful retreat to guests desiring an escape to the country for a relaxing weekend.

The cabin is located eight miles from Nacogdoches. If you like fun shopping and quaint restaurants, you'll absolutely love visiting the oldest town in Texas! If outdoor activities call to you, fishing and boating on Sam Rayburn Reservoir, the state's largest lake, is within a short drive. And the Piney Woods of East Texas offer miles of hiking trails and great bird watching.

If you are fortunate enough to be in Nacogdoches in June you can eat all the blueberries you want at the Blueberry Festival.

INNKEEPERS:	Stan and Christie Cook
ADDRESS:	4741 County Road 724, Nacogdoches, Texas 75964
TELEPHONE:	(936) 559-1125; (936) 615-1150 cell
E-MAIL:	reservations@fairbreezecottage.com
WEBSITE:	www.fairbreezecottage.com
ROOMS:	1 Cottage; Private bath
CHILDREN:	Unable to accommodate
PETS:	Not allowed

Bacon Spinach Quiche

Makes 6 Servings

Serve with fruit for breakfast or with a green salad for lunch or dinner. This recipe can easily be doubled for larger groups.

8 ounces bacon
1 (9-inch) regular-size pie shell
   (thawed or homemade)
6 eggs
½ cup sour cream (light or regular)
½ (10-ounce) package frozen spinach,
   chopped, cooked and drained well
1 cup (4 ounces) grated Colby/Jack cheese
   (light or regular)
Salt and pepper, to taste

Preheat oven to 350°F. Cook bacon until crisp. Drain on paper towels (reserve a little of the bacon grease and brush it onto the bottom of the pie shell—this adds a lot of flavor). Crumble the bacon into the pie shell.

In a large bowl, beat eggs and sour cream together. Pour the egg mixture over the bacon in the pie shell. Spread the spinach over the egg mixture. Spread the cheese over the spinach. Season with salt and pepper. Bake for 45 minutes, or until the top of the quiche is golden brown. Cool for 10 minutes before slicing and serving.

BAILEY'S UPTOWN INN

In the exclusive uptown neighborhood of Dallas, Bailey's Uptown Inn is a classic new structure built to blend with the surrounding 1920s historic community charm. The inn is within walking distance of some of the best restaurants and shops in town. The trolley system serving uptown and downtown Dallas is less than a block away.

The combination of elegant décor, homey atmosphere, and friendly but unobtrusive service at Bailey's Uptown Inn appeals to both visitors and business travelers. The hospitable innkeepers do not have the surname Bailey. The inn actually takes its name from the innkeeper's dear departed dog named Bailey. All of the rooms are well equipped with modern conveniences. Several rooms have a fireplace, private porch, and a whirlpool bath.

Specialties often prepared for the full breakfast on weekends include French toast stuffed with cream cheese and strawberries, southwestern frittatas, and cloud cakes. A Continental breakfast is served on weekdays.

INNKEEPER:	Andrea Hundley
ADDRESS:	2505 Worthington Street, Dallas, Texas 75204
MAILING:	(2807 Allen Street #808) 75204
TELEPHONE:	(214) 720-2258; (214) 292-9557
E-MAIL:	info@baileysuptowninn.com
WEBSITE:	www.baileysuptowninn.com
ROOMS:	5 Rooms; Private baths
CHILDREN:	Unable to accommodate
PETS:	Not permitted

FETA AND BASIL FRITTATA

Makes 4 Servings

*"This dish is pretty light and healthy. I cut it into wedges
and serve with polish kielbasa, or turkey sausage and fruit."*
—INNKEEPER, *Bailey's Uptown Inn*

1–2 tablespoons bacon grease or butter
(using 2 omelet pans, each pan will need
1 tablespoon, if pan has a non-stick coating
this can be reduced to ½ tablespoon)
12 eggs
4 tablespoons basil, chopped
4 teaspoons sun dried tomatoes, drained, chopped
4 tablespoons feta cheese, shredded

Heat broiler. Using 2 small omelet pans, heat bacon grease or
melt butter in the pans on the stovetop.

In a bowl, beat eggs; pour evenly into the 2 heated omelet pans.
As eggs begin to cook, add basil. Pull cooked edges up to let liquid
underneath while cooking. Add feta cheese to the egg mixture;
add sun-dried tomatoes. When most of the liquid is cooked, put
pans under broiler, just until eggs are firm. Take out of oven. Slide
out of pan onto plate; slice and serve.

TIP:
Feta cheese is very salty. Do not add additional salt.

WRIGLEY HOUSE
BED AND BREAKFAST

There has been a dwelling on the Wrigley House location since 1883 when the lot was incorporated in the Old Town Survey, but according to Sanborn historical maps, the present dwelling appeared sometime between 1912 and 1920. The house is a beautiful example of the era.

Located only two blocks from historic downtown Brenham with its antique stores, shops, and restaurants, it is the perfect base for exploring the Bluebonnet or Independence trails, and for access to Round Top Antique Fairs and the many local festivals. The Blue Bell Creamery, and the Monastery of St. Claire's Miniature Horses are popular tourist destinations.

The host uses local produce and products whenever possible—so look for Chappell Hill sausages, fresh vegetables, and eggs from free-range chickens (kept by neighbors) on your breakfast platter.

Corporate travelers will enjoy wireless Internet connection and free local and national phone calls.

INNKEEPER:	Marilynn Wrigley
ADDRESS:	506 South Park, Brenham, Texas 77833
TELEPHONE:	(979) 836-4346 phone and fax
E-MAIL:	info@wrigleyhouse.com
WEBSITE:	www.wrigleyhouse.com
ROOMS:	2 Rooms; 1 Cottage; Private baths
CHILDREN:	Ages 12 and older are welcome
PETS:	Not permitted

Sausage and Hash Brown Mini-Frittatas

Makes 24–30 Frittatas

1 pound bulk pork sausage
1 large onion, chopped
2 cups frozen hash browns, thawed
1 cup cheddar cheese, grated
3 tablespoons all-purpose flour
8 eggs, beaten
1 cup Ranch-style salad dressing
½ cup milk
Salsa as accompaniment

Preheat oven to 325°F. Grease enough muffin tins to accommodate 24–30 frittatas. In a large skillet, sauté the sausage and onion over medium heat, cooking until pork is no longer pink. Drain the sausage; let cool. In a large mixing bowl, combine sausage, onion, potatoes, and cheese. Toss to mix. Stir in flour. Add the eggs, salad dressing, and milk; stir well. Spoon the mixture into muffin tins, filling each halfway. Bake for 15–20 minutes, or until frittatas are set and golden brown. Turn out onto plates; serve with warm salsa.

Brazos
Bed and Breakfast

"Where the Brazos River meets up with the History of Texas"

Situated on ten rolling acres, Brazos Bed and Breakfast is in the town of Washington, just two miles from the birthplace of Texas. Follow the winding road from the inn to the secluded grove

of lush, live oaks and you will discover one of the most serene spots in Washington County.

Two exceptional suites are offered at the Brazos. Both suites include a butler's pantry, Dish TV, wireless Internet service, and a full bathroom. Enter the enchanting Tree Top Suite from your private balcony and outdoor dining area. The roomy Texan Suite extends outdoors onto a large back patio complete with a romantic arbor, a fire pit, a gas grill, and a view of the organic garden. After you have had a wonderful night's sleep on Egyptian cotton sheets, your morning begins with a generous breakfast delivered to your door in a basket.

"Wow! What an awesome experience! I came here with my mother but I'll be back with my husband!" —GUEST

INNKEEPER:	Diane Hunter
ADDRESS:	20251 Pickens Road, Washington, Texas 787880
TELEPHONE:	(936) 878-2230 phone and fax
E-MAIL:	dianebrazosbb@sbcglobal.net
WEBSITE:	www. brazosbedandbreakfast.com
ROOMS:	2 Suites; Private baths
CHILDREN:	Unable to accommodate
PETS:	Not allowed; Resident chickens and cows

Fire-Roasted Green Chili Frittata

Makes 6 Servings

"This egg dish isn't spicy, but it is flavorful."
—INNKEEPER, *Brazos Bed and Breakfast*

6 slices of bacon or ½ pound pork sausage
1 tablespoon butter or oil for sautéing
¼ cup green onion, thinly sliced
$\frac{1}{3}$ cup red bell pepper, diced
6 large eggs
1 cup Colby Jack cheese, divided
1 can (4-ounce) fire-roasted green chilies, diced
¼ teaspoon salt
¼ teaspoon course ground pepper

Preheat oven to 350°F. Spray a 9-inch glass pie plate with vegetable oil. In a skillet, fry the bacon or sausage; set aside to cool. When cool, break or cut into small pieces. In a skillet add butter, onion, and red bell pepper. Sauté until soft. In a medium bowl, beat eggs; add ¾ cup cheese, green chilies, salt and pepper. Add bacon, onion and red bell pepper. Pour mixture into a 9-inch pie plate. Bake for 20 minutes; don't overcook. Remove from oven, sprinkle with remaining cheese and cover with a plate for 5 minutes. Serve with a side of salsa.

AUSTIN'S STAR OF TEXAS INN

One of Austin's most treasured historic buildings is home to Austin's Star of Texas Inn. The University of Texas tower can be seen from some of the upstairs bedrooms in this beautiful Victorian central Austin home. Five of the nine guestrooms have either a private porch or direct access to the wrap-around veranda on the second floor. Most of the rooms offer claw-foot bathtubs for a leisurely, tension-reducing evening soak. High-speed Internet access, private phone lines, an on-site fax machine, and photocopier are available for the business traveler.

Wide glass double doors open into a gorgeous dining room that will easily seat sixteen people. The dining room also has an entrance to the front porch where a table is set for outdoor dining if you prefer. A sweet dish, a savory dish, fresh fruit, bagels, and more are provided to ensure that the morning fare will satisfy your appetite. The coffee is always hot and breakfast is always good at Austin's Star of Texas Inn.

INNKEEPERS:	Sylvia and Chris Mackey
ADDRESS:	611 West 22nd Street, Austin, Texas 78705
TELEPHONE:	(512) 477-9639; (866) 472-6700
E-MAIL:	sylvia@austinfolkhouse.com
WEBSITE:	www.staroftexasinn.com
ROOMS:	10 Rooms; Private baths
CHILDREN:	Ages 12 and older are welcome
PETS:	Not permitted

Vegetable Frittata

Makes 12 Servings

*"Any or all of the vegetables in the ingredients list may be used.
The choice is yours—but they need to be fresh."*
—INNKEEPER, *Austin's Star of Texas*

Olive oil for sautéing
½ cup mushrooms, sliced
½ cup tomato, chopped
½ cup bell pepper, diced
½ cup spinach, chopped
½ cup broccoli, chopped
½ cup carrots, shredded
½ cup sun-dried tomatoes, chopped
½ cup onion, diced
½–1 whole jalapeno, chopped
Fresh basil, to taste
1–2 cups cheese (choose your favorite)
½ cup fresh Parmesan (optional)
Sprigs of fresh basil
Salt and freshly ground black pepper, to taste
12 eggs

Preheat oven to 375°F. In a large ovenproof skillet, sauté vegetables in olive oil over medium heat. Start with the vegetables that require the most cooking time, such as bell pepper, carrots, broccoli, zucchini, onions. Finish up with tomatoes, mushrooms and spinach. Once tender, turn off the heat. Add basil, cheeses, salt and pepper. Mix together to spread evenly throughout the pan.

In a medium bowl, beat eggs. Pour the eggs over the vegetable mixture. Make sure there is enough olive oil still in the pan so that the eggs will not stick. Put the pan in the oven and bake for 30 minutes or until there is no liquid in the middle.

CREEKHAVEN INN

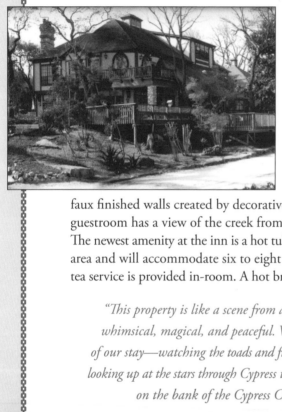

The banks of Cypress Creek form the natural setting for the Creekhaven Inn. Guests are welcome to wade in the spring-fed creek or take a walk through the ancient cypress grove on the grounds of this Texas Hill Country bed and breakfast. Shopping and dining in the downtown Wimberley Village Square is just two blocks from the quietly positioned inn.

Throughout the interior of Creekhaven, artistic works from various local artists are on display. Each of the thirteen guestrooms has warm faux finished walls created by decorative artist Denice Calley. Every guestroom has a view of the creek from a private deck or balcony. The newest amenity at the inn is a hot tub that is located in the garden area and will accommodate six to eight people. Gourmet coffee and tea service is provided in-room. A hot breakfast is served buffet style.

"This property is like a scene from an enchanted fairytale—whimsical, magical, and peaceful. We enjoyed every moment of our stay—watching the toads and frogs hop across the pathways, looking up at the stars through Cypress treetops, and drinking coffee on the bank of the Cypress Creek." —GUEST

INNKEEPERS:	Bill and Pat Appleman
ADDRESS:	400 Mill Race Lane, Wimberley, Texas 78676
TELEPHONE:	(512) 847-9344; (800) 827-1913
E-MAIL:	pat@creekhaveninn.com
WEBSITE:	www.creekhaveninn.com
ROOMS:	12 Rooms; 2 Suites; Private baths
CHILDREN:	Ages 16 and older are welcome
PETS:	Not permitted

Migas Frittata

Makes 4 to 6 Servings

1 tablespoon butter
½ medium yellow onion, diced
½ red pepper, diced
1 small jalapeño, minced (optional)
1 cup Tostito chips, lightly crushed
6 eggs
½ cup fresh pico de gallo
    (sold prepared at most grocery stores)
½ cup cheddar cheese, shredded
1 teaspoon water
½ teaspoon fajita seasoning
½ teaspoon dried cilantro

Preheat oven to 350°F. Using a nonstick ovenproof frying pan, sauté butter, onions, pepper, and jalapeno on medium heat until soft. Add lightly crushed Tostito chips; stir until lightly browned and crisped. Sprinkle well-drained pico de gallo over ingredients in frying pan. Top with cheese.

In a medium bowl, whisk together eggs, water, fajita seasoning and dried cilantro. Add whisked egg mixture to the frying pan and remove immediately from stovetop and place directly in oven. Bake for 30 minutes until puffed, firm, and lightly browned.

Remove from oven. Let stand for 5 minutes. Cut into wedges; serve with salsa or pico de gallo, and flour tortillas.

THE GAZEBO

The Gazebo Bed & Breakfast is a two-story, Georgian-style home designed and built by innkeepers Clyde and Janet McMurray in 1981. As educators, your on-site innkeepers have an appreciation of American history and have spent many years acquiring American Empire and Victorian antique furniture to compliment family heirlooms.

In the foyer, you will be greeted by a 20-foot ceiling and a beautiful French crystal chandelier. The antique-filled parlor and the elegant dining room each have a fireplace.

In the morning, coffee or tea in silver service will be awaiting you outside your door, or you may prefer to leisurely relax in the screened-in back porch furnished with turn-of-the-century wicker. A full gourmet breakfast in a Victorian setting will be served in the authentic antique furnished dining room.

The innkeepers strive to offer guests comfort, privacy, relaxation and Southern hospitality in a small, rural, Texas Main Street town.

INNKEEPERS: Clyde and Janet McMurray

ADDRESS: 906 Sessions Street, Bowie, Texas 76230

TELEPHONE: (940) 872-4852

E-MAIL: info@gazebobnb.com

WEBSITE: www.gazebobnb.com

ROOMS: 4 Rooms; Private & shared baths

CHILDREN: Age 12 and older welcome

PETS: Not allowed; Resident cat

Mediterranean Egg Soufflé

Makes 4 Servings

"We serve this delicious egg dish as a double entrée with French toast or Belgian waffles, although it could easily be an entrée on its own. It always gets rave reviews!"
This dish needs to be refrigerated overnight.
—INNKEEPER, *The Gazebo.*

2–3 slices white bread, crusts removed
2 tablespoons butter, melted
1 (3-ounce) package cream cheese, cut into small pieces
3 ounces feta cheese, crumbled
12 ounces ham, cubed
1½ cups (6 ounces) sharp cheddar cheese, grated
¼ cup (2 ounces) mozzarella cheese, grated
4 medium eggs, slightly beaten
½ cup half & half
1 teaspoon all-purpose Greek seasoning
1 teaspoon Coleman's dry mustard
1½ tablespoons chopped chives
Parsley sprigs for garnish

Spray an 8x8-inch baking dish with nonstick cooking spray. Tear bread into pieces and place in bottom of dish. Pour melted butter over bread. Sprinkle cream cheese pieces and crumbled feta cheese over bread. Sprinkle ham and then cheddar and mozzarella cheeses on top.

In a medium bowl, combine eggs, half & half, Greek seasoning, and dry mustard. Beat until well mixed and pour evenly over the cheese. Sprinkle chives on top. Cover and refrigerate overnight.

The next morning, preheat oven to 350°F. Bake for 50–60 minutes, or until mixture is set. Let stand for 5 minutes before serving. Garnish each serving with a sprig of fresh parsley.

Pancakes, Waffles, & French Toast

Pancakes, Waffles, & French Toast

He who goes to bed hungry,

dreams of pancakes.

—ANONYMOUS

MEMORY LANE

Just 56 miles from San Antonio, this is a great getaway for locals and tourists alike. Spend the day seeing the sights in the city and then retreat to Memory Lane to be pampered and rest weary feet.

This guest's lovely verse tells us everything we need to know about Memory Lane.

> *"Enthusiastic smiles, warmly accommodating,*
> *flowers, mints, coffee and tea, muffins and apple pancakes,*
> *sunning by the pool, delightful conversation, caring suggestions,*
> *   sharing thoughts,*
> *a few days in time to share and cherish down Memory—Memory Lane."*
>
> —JENNIFER AND PHIL, Houston, Texas

INNKEEPER: Janet Morgan

ADDRESS: 403 K.C. Memory Lane, Dripping Springs, Texas 78620

MAILING: (PO Box 803) 78620

TELEPHONE: (512) 894-0700; (512) 905-2787

E-MAIL: janetmorgan@hughes.net

WEBSITE: www.memorylanebedandbreakfast.com

ROOMS: 2 Suites; Private baths

CHILDREN: Welcome

PETS: Not Allowed; Resident goats, chickens, donkey, horse, and cats

Puffed Pancake
with Summer Fruit

Makes 2 Servings

"I use local organically-grown fruit and Paula's Orange Liqueur
also locally made—great for Sunday morning mimosas."
—INNKEEPER, *Memory Lane*

⅓ cup white flour (organic, if possible)

2 tablespoons sugar

⅓ cup milk

3 eggs (range-free, if possible)

¼ cup unsalted butter

2 firm ripe peaches, sliced

½ pint blueberries

or

1½ cups raspberries or blackberries

2 tablespoons brown sugar

¼ cup orange liqueur (your favorite)

Confectioner's sugar, to sprinkle on top

Whipped Cream, to garnish

Preheat oven to 425°F. In a medium bowl, mix flour, sugar, milk, and eggs until thoroughly blended. Set aside.

In a 10- or 12-inch ovenproof frying pan, melt butter over medium heat; add fruit, and brown sugar. Stir often until fruit is slightly softened. Add liqueur and heat through for 3–5 more minutes. Remove from heat.

Pour egg mixture over fruit and immediately put in oven. Bake 18 minutes until puffy and golden brown. Remove pancake from oven; flip onto a large plate; sprinkle with confectioner's sugar. Serve whipped cream on the side.

THE INN OF MANY FACES

Set on two acres of towering pine trees, the Inn of Many Faces was built in 1897 by J.B. McDougall, one of Denison's founding fathers. Recently restored, the house is now a comfortable retreat lovingly managed by Charlie and Gloria Morton.

When you enter the inn through the foyer, you know from the start that you are staying at someplace special. Feel free to read from the "Wall of Quotations."

Each room is a delight, and you will want a tour of each. Katy's Room is the most beautiful; Texoma is the largest; Cabbage Rose is reminiscent of your grandma's house; and the English Garden has the best views of the garden and gazebo.

Surprises await you at every turn. Whether enjoying the garden or soaking in the whirlpool tub, the inn's collection of whimsical faces greet you—hence the name "The Inn of Many Faces."

INNKEEPERS: Charlie and Gloria Morton

ADDRESS: 412 West Morton Street, Denison, Texas 75020

TELEPHONE: (903) 465-4639

E-MAIL: BandB@innofmanyfaces.com

WEBSITE: www.innofmanyfaces.com

ROOMS: 4 Rooms; Private baths

CHILDREN: Age 11 and older welcome

PETS: Not allowed

Baked German Apple Pancake

Makes 5 Servings

"A favorite dish of our guests!"
—INNKEEPER, *Inn of Many Faces*

APPLE MIXTURE:

2 tablespoons butter

½ cup white sugar

½ cup brown sugar

2 teaspoons ground cinnamon

¼ teaspoon salt

3 large Granny Smith apples,
   peeled, cored and sliced

PANCAKE BATTER:

6 eggs, beaten

1 cup milk

1 cup flour

2 teaspoons white sugar

¼ teaspoon salt

3 tablespoons butter, melted

For the apple mixture: Preheat oven to 450°F. Spray five 5-inch diameter ramekins (the ramekins should each have a 1½-cup capacity) with nonstick cooking spray. In a skillet, melt butter over medium-low heat. Stir in the butter, white sugar, brown sugar, cinnamon and salt. Add the apple and cook until slightly soft (avoid letting the mixture boil to keep the sugar from crystallizing). Divide the apples equally among the ramekins.

For the pancake batter: In a large bowl, mix all of the pancake batter ingredients, stirring just until combined (the batter will be lumpy). Pour over the top of the apple mixture in each ramekin.

Bake for 18 minutes. Lower oven temperature to 350°F and bake for 7–10 more minutes. Serve. (You do not need additional syrup for serving as the apple mixture makes its own syrup during baking.)

Brackenridge House

Brackenridge House innkeeper Bennie Blansett is a retired Air Force Colonel. His wife, Sue, left her job as a university administrator when they launched their second career as innkeepers. They are native Texans who chose to retire in San Antonio after living all over the United States, Guam, the Philippines, and Germany.

The Blansetts can tell you stories of the way San Antonio used to be. Both are well versed on places to go in San Antonio and the Texas Hill Country.

While you are staying in this historic, San Antonio, King William bed and breakfast, located on a peaceful tree-lined residential street, you will have all the advantages of being near the River Walk, the trolley, the Alamo, the convention center, El Mercado and the Alamodome, but without the noise and congestion. Wonderful neighborhood restaurants close by offer delicious meals without the River Walk crowds.

Don't forget about the hot tub in the rear garden area during the winter months. It is the perfect place to soak your tired muscles and aching feet after a busy day of sightseeing.

INNKEEPERS:	Bennie and Sue Blansett
ADDRESS:	230 Madison, San Antonio, Texas 78204
TELEPHONE:	(210) 271-3442; (800) 221-1412; (210) 226-3139 fax
E-MAIL:	brackenridgebb@aol.com
WEBSITE:	www.brackenridgehouse.com
ROOMS:	2 Rooms; 3 Suites; 1 Cottage; 1 Carriage House; Private baths
CHILDREN:	Welcome in cottage; Age 12 and older in main house
PETS:	Allowed in cottage and carriage house

French-Baked Pancake

Makes 8 Large Servings
Beautiful presentation—great taste!

PANCAKE BATTER:

1 stick (½ cup) butter,
room temperature, plus
3 tablespoons butter, melted

4 tablespoons sugar

3 eggs plus 2 eggs

2 cups flour

1½ teaspoons baking powder

1¼ cups milk

3 cups small curd cottage cheese

1 teaspoon salt

BLUEBERRY SAUCE:

1 (21-ounce) can blueberry pie filling

¾ cup blueberry syrup (about ½ of a 12-ounce bottle)

SOUR CREAM SAUCE:

1 cup sour cream

1 teaspoon vanilla extract

2 tablespoons powdered sugar

Grated zest of 1 orange, for garnish

For the pancake: Preheat oven to 350°F. Spray a 9x13-inch baking pan with nonstick cooking spray. In a large bowl, combine the 1 stick of butter and sugar. Add 3 eggs; beat well. Combine flour and baking powder. Mix flour mixture and milk alternately into butter mixture. Pour ½ of batter in pan.

In a medium bowl, mix cottage cheese, 2 eggs, the 3 tablespoons melted butter, and salt. Spread over the batter in the pan. Top with remaining batter. Bake for 60 minutes, or until golden brown.

For the blueberry and sour cream sauce: In a saucepan, mix and heat blueberry pie filling and syrup together to make a blueberry sauce. In a small bowl, mix sour cream, vanilla extract, and powdered sugar to make a sour cream sauce.

Cut baked pancake into squares. Serve with blueberry sauce and a dollop of sour cream sauce. Sprinkle with orange zest.

Vieh's Bed and Breakfast

"Where you come as a guest and leave as a friend."

Experience the friendly hospitality of south Texas in this comfortable ranch-style home on 15 acres, just three miles from Old Mexico, and centrally located between Brownsville, Santa Ana and Laguna Atascosa. A 10-acre pond across the back of the property offers a relaxed walking area and the opportunity to view a variety of area wildlife.

There are two butterfly gardens on the property where you can see such beauties as Pixies, Giant Swallowtails, and Admirals.

INNKEEPERS:	Lana and Charles Vieh
ADDRESS:	18413 Landrum Park Road, San Benito, Texas 78586
TELEPHONE:	(956) 425-4651
E-MAIL:	viehbb@aol.com
WEBSITE:	www.vieh.com
ROOMS:	4 Rooms; 1 Cottage; Private and shared baths
CHILDREN:	Welcome
PETS:	Welcome; call head; Resident parrots and horses

Lana's Cornmeal Pancakes

Makes 4 Servings (12 Pancakes)

1 cup whole-wheat flour
1 cup yellow cornmeal
1 tablespoon baking powder
1 teaspoon baking soda
1 tablespoon sugar
1½ cups buttermilk
¼ cup cooking oil
1 egg, separated
Syrup, for serving

In a large bowl, sift together whole-wheat flour, cornmeal, baking powder, baking soda and sugar. In a medium bowl, combine buttermilk, oil and egg yolk; add to the dry ingredients; mix until just moistened. In another bowl, beat egg white until stiff; gently fold into batter (small bits of egg white will still be visible). (If a thinner batter is desired, add up to ½ cup more buttermilk.)

Preheat a lightly greased griddle or skillet over medium heat. Spoon batter onto griddle. Cook until pancakes are golden on both sides. The pancakes are done when golden. Serve with syrup.

STAR OF TEXAS

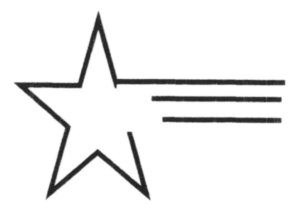

The Wildrose Retreat at the Star of Texas is a little house built in 1908. The innkeepers moved the house to their property and restored it as a private retreat for the guests of the inn. The house has a spacious sitting room, kitchenette, and a large bath with a two-person Jacuzzi tub. A stairway leads to a loft bedroom with a queen-size iron bed. Double French doors lead out to a sitting deck to enjoy the sunrise or a quiet evening under the stars.

If you are looking for a wedding destination, the Star of Texas is a perfect choice. Outdoor decks surrounded by native gardens, or the Garden Chapel that can accommodate 60 people are two choices often picked by the bride.

INNKEEPERS: Don and Debbie Morelock

ADDRESS: 650 Morelock Lane, Brownwood, Texas 76801

TELEPHONE: (325) 646-4128; (800) 850-2003

E-MAIL: relaxing@star-of-texas.com

WEBSITE: www.star-of-texas.com

ROOMS: 5 Cottages; 1 Tipi; Private baths

CHILDREN: Unable to accommodate

PETS: Call ahead; Resident pets

Fall Pancakes
with Apple Spice Syrup

Makes 4 Servings

*"These pancakes are great for crisp fall mornings.
Top with fresh whipped cream and serve with bacon."*
—INNKEEPER, *Star of Texas*

2 cups whole-wheat baking mix
   (such as Hodgson Mill Insta-Bake mix)
½ teaspoon cinnamon
2 eggs
1¼ cups milk
½ cup applesauce
1 teaspoon vanilla extract
Whipped cream and chopped pecans, for garnish
Apple spice syrup (recipe follows)

In a medium bowl, combine baking mix and cinnamon. In another bowl, combine eggs, milk, applesauce, and vanilla extract; add to dry ingredients and stir until combined. Preheat a greased griddle or skillet over medium heat. Spoon batter by ¼-cupfuls onto griddle. Cook until pancakes are golden on both sides. Serve pancakes topped with whipped cream and sprinkled with pecans. Offer warm apple spice syrup on the side.

APPLE SPICE SYRUP:
¼ cup brown sugar
2 tablespoons cornstarch
¼ teaspoon cinnamon
⅛ teaspoon nutmeg
1½ cups apple juice

In a medium saucepan, combine brown sugar, cornstarch, cinnamon, and nutmeg.

Gradually stir in apple juice until smooth. Stirring constantly, bring to a boil over medium heat. Boil for 1 minute, until the mixture thickens. Remove from heat. Serve warm. (The syrup can be prepared ahead, covered and refrigerated. Gently reheat syrup in the microwave or on the stove when ready to use).

THE COTTON PALACE

The Cotton Palace lavishes guests with fine furnishings in comfortable and spacious guest areas. Cozy up with a book in front of the original green stone fireplace, or help yourself to a variety of beverages and homemade treats from the bottomless cookie jar.

A full gourmet breakfast is served in the dramatic red dining room. House specialties include fresh seasonal fruit in champagne wine sauce, crème brulée French toast, and lemon soufflé pancakes with blueberries.

Attractions close to the inn include Baylor University, the Texas Ranger Museum, and the Texas Sports Hall of Fame.

INNKEEPERS: Becky Hodges and Dutch & Betty Schroeder
ADDRESS: 1910 Austin Avenue, Waco, Texas 76701
TELEPHONE: (254) 753-7294; (877) 632-2312; (254) 753-7921 fax
E-MAIL: cotnpalace@aol.com
WEBSITE: www.thecottonpalace.com
ROOMS: 4 Rooms; 2 Suites; 1 Cottage; Private baths
CHILDREN: Age 12 and older welcome
PETS: Not allowed

Crisp Waffles

Makes 4 Servings

*"There are hundreds of waffle recipes—believe me,
I've tried them all—but these are the best!"*
—INNKEEPER, *The Cotton Palace*

¾ cup flour
¼ cup cornstarch
½ teaspoon salt
½ teaspoon baking powder
¼ teaspoon baking soda
¾ cup buttermilk
¼ cup milk
6 tablespoons vegetable oil
1 large egg, separated
1 tablespoon sugar
½ teaspoon vanilla extract

Preheat oven to 200°F. Preheat a lightly greased waffle iron. In a medium bowl, mix flour, cornstarch, salt, baking powder, and baking soda. In a small bowl, combine buttermilk, milk, oil, and egg yolk; add to dry ingredients and whisk until just mixed.

In a small bowl, beat egg white almost to soft peaks. Sprinkle in sugar; beat until peaks are firm and glossy. Beat in vanilla. Drop beaten egg white into batter in dollops. Gently fold in egg white with a rubber spatula until just incorporated. Spoon batter onto hot waffle iron; bake until crisp and nutty brown. Remove waffle and set it directly on the oven rack to keep it warm and crisp. Repeat with remaining batter. (To keep waffles crisp, do not stack them.) Serve with syrup.

VARIATIONS:
Cranberry Orange Waffles: Stir 2 teaspoons finely grated orange zest and ½ cup coarsely chopped dried cranberries into the batter.

Chocolate Chip Waffles: Stir ½ cup coarsely chopped chocolate chips or ½ cup mini chocolate chips into the batter.

Cornmeal Waffles: Substitute ½ cup cornmeal for ½ cup of the flour.

SOUTHERN ROSE RANCH

"Welcome to the Ranch!
Where a good rain and a new calf are always welcome."

A visitor to Southern Rose Ranch will get a glimpse of a simpler life and a slower pace. This is very much a working country ranch. The ranch breeds Belted Galloway cattle, also known as Oreo Cows or Texas Zebras. Their appearance is quite unusual.

Your stay at the ranch will include a gourmet breakfast made with farm-fresh eggs and herbs served in your private suite or in the outdoor kitchen.

This storybook ranch is perfect for the romantic couple's weekend or a "girlfriend getaway."

"We loved everything! Particularly the wonderful breakfasts, pastoral scenes, animals, warm and friendly hosts, the spa, and rooms well-equipped and beautifully decorated." —GUESTS

INNKEEPERS: Donna and Steve Cummins

ADDRESS: 8580 Dairy Farm Road. Chappell Hill, Texas 77426

TELEPHONE: (979) 251-7871; (979) 251-4028 cell

E-MAIL: stay@SouthernRoseRanch.com

WEBSITE: www.SouthernRoseRanch.com

ROOMS: 2 Suites; Private baths

CHILDREN: Unable to accommodate

PETS: Not allowed; Resident pets

Waffles a la Orange

Makes 4 to 5 Servings

"This is a pretty breakfast with a light orange flavor and a simple drizzle that is a new twist on syrup."
—INNKEEPER, *Southern Rose Ranch*

WAFFLES:
3 cups of Krusteuz Belgian Waffle Mix
      or any other prepackaged waffle mix
2 eggs
⅓ cup oil
½ cup water
1 cup orange juice
1 tablespoon triple sec
1 tablespoon zest of orange

DRIZZLE:
¼ cup orange juice
¼ cup corn syrup
Powdered sugar, to dust tops of waffles

Preheat a lightly greased waffle iron. In a large bowl, combine waffle mix, eggs, oil, water, and orange juice; blend well. Add triple sec and zest of orange. Stir to mix in thoroughly. Cook waffles in waffle iron.

While waffles are cooking, prepare drizzle. In small bowl, combine orange juice and corn syrup. Pour drizzle into a serving cup. Remove waffles from waffle iron; dust with powdered sugar and serve with drizzle on the side.

> *A waffle is a pancake*
>
> *with a syrup trap.*
>
> —MITCH HEDBERG

THE HUNTER ROAD STAGECOACH STOP

STAGECOACH STOP
Bed and Breakfast

Lovingly resorted to its original design, this historic homestead is thought to be Bonito, a Stagecoach Stop and one time post office of the settlement known as Stringtown. Here you will find another era as you pass through the doors of the Log Pen Cabins, which were erected in 1848. Warmly decorated cedar-beamed rooms fragrant with the scent of herbs hold a wealth of antiques.

This is the ideal spot for travelers desiring a picturesque landscape in which to enjoy gardens of antique roses, herbs and native plants. The innkeeper, a landscape designer, welcomes you personally to this little bit of heaven redolent of early Texas.

A gourmet breakfast is served in the fragrant rose garden, on the breezy porches or in the cozy dining room of the main house.

INNKEEPERS:	Bettina and Jeff Messinger
ADDRESS:	5441 FM 1102, New Braunfels, Texas 78132
TELEPHONE:	(830) 620-9453
E-MAIL:	stagecoach@satx.rr.com
WEBSITE:	www.stagecoachbedandbreakfast.com
ROOMS:	4 Rooms; 1 Suite; 4 Cottages; Private baths
CHILDREN:	Welcome
PETS:	Call ahead. Resident dog, cat & rabbits

Yeast Waffles

Makes 6 to 8 Servings (12 to 16 Waffles)

*"Make the batter for these waffles the night before serving.
This is one of our guests' favorites. It's best made with a Belgian
waffle maker. I sometimes add fresh strawberries,
whipped cream and chopped pecans."*
—INNKEEPER, *Hunter Road Stagecoach Stop*

1 envelope (2½ teaspoons) active dry yeast

¼ cup warm water (105–115ºF)

1 teaspoon plus 1 tablespoon sugar

2 cups warm milk (105–115ºF)

1 stick (½ cup) butter, melted

2 cups flour

¼ teaspoon salt

2 eggs, lightly beaten

¼ teaspoon baking soda

Fresh strawberries, sliced (optional)

Whipped cream, for garnish (optional)

Chopped pecans, for garnish (optional)

Syrup, for serving

Stir the yeast into warm water. Stir in 1 teaspoon of sugar. Let
stand for 10 minutes (if the mixture foams and grows in volume,
the yeast is active and ready to use).

Pour the warm milk into a large bowl. Add melted butter, flour,
salt and 1 tablespoon of sugar; stir thoroughly. Stir in the yeast
mixture. Put the batter into a large container with a tight fitting
lid (the batter will double in size—be sure the container is large
enough). Leave the container on the counter overnight.

The next morning, stir in the eggs and baking soda. Bake the
waffles in a preheated, lightly greased waffle iron. Top with strawberries, whipped cream and pecans, if desired. Serve with syrup.

BAILEY'S UPTOWN INN

In the exclusive uptown neighborhood of Dallas, Bailey's Uptown Inn is a classic new structure built to blend with the surrounding 1920s historic community charm. The inn is within walking distance of some of the best restaurants and shops in town. The trolley system serving uptown and downtown Dallas is less than a block away.

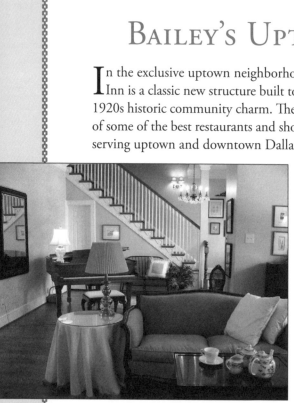

The combination of elegant décor, homey atmosphere, and friendly but unobtrusive service at Bailey's Uptown Inn appeals to both visitors and business travelers. The hospitable innkeepers do not have the surname Bailey. The inn actually takes its name from the innkeeper's dear departed dog named Bailey. All of the rooms are well equipped with modern conveniences. Several rooms have a fireplace, private porch, and a whirlpool bath.

Specialties often prepared for the full breakfast on weekends include French toast stuffed with cream cheese and strawberries, southwestern frittatas, and cloud cakes. A Continental breakfast is served on weekdays.

INNKEEPER:	Andrea Hundley
ADDRESS:	2505 Worthington Street, Dallas, Texas 75204
MAILING:	(2807 Allen Street #808) 75204
TELEPHONE:	(214) 720-2258; (214) 292-9557
E-MAIL:	info@baileysuptowninn.com
WEBSITE:	www.baileysuptowninn.com
ROOMS:	5 Rooms; Private baths
CHILDREN:	Unable to accommodate
PETS:	Not permitted

Croissant French Toast

Makes 8 Servings

*"This dish is always a big hit, and while it doesn't look
like a big serving, it is very rich and buttery.
I usually serve it with bacon and fruit."*
—INNKEEPER, *Bailey's Uptown Inn*

FRENCH TOAST:

8 day-old croissants (or from the freezer)

8 ounces cream cheese

3 tablespoons jam or marmalade

6 eggs

1½ cups milk

1 teaspoon vanilla

½ teaspoon cinnamon

Pinch of nutmeg

Butter for griddle

Powdered sugar, to dust tops of French toast

SYRUP:

1 cup sugar

½ cup water

¾ cup orange juice

1 tablespoon cornstarch

For the French toast croissants: Heat large frying pan or griddle to
medium. Slice croissants in half and spread with cream cheese and
jam. In a medium bowl, mix eggs, milk, vanilla, cinnamon and
nutmeg. Dunk croissants in the egg mixture. Croissants should be
soggy. Melt butter on griddle and fry croissants. When they are
cooked through, remove from griddle and dust with powdered
sugar. Serve with syrup.

For the syrup: In a small saucepan, combine sugar and water
and heat until sugar is dissolved. In a small bowl, mix orange
and cornstarch; add to sugar water; heat until thickened.

ROSEVINE INN

Experience the old-fashioned concept of a bed and breakfast at the Rosevine Inn. Guest accommodations are cheerfully decorated, and each room has a private bath. The bed and breakfast is furnished with antiques and country collectibles.

The barn/game room is furnished in 1930s hunting lodge decor. A stone floor, fireplace, pub table, trophy heads and hides, and period furnishings complete the setting.

INNKEEPERS:	Rebecca and Bert Powell
ADDRESS:	415 South Vine, Tyler, Texas 75702
TELEPHONE:	(903) 592-2221; (903) 592-5522
E-MAIL:	info@rosevine.com
WEBSITE:	www.rosevine.com
ROOMS:	6 Rooms; 1 Suite; 2 Cottages; Private baths
CHILDREN:	Age 5 and older welcome
PETS:	Not allowed; Resident outdoor cats

Banana French Toast

Makes 2 to 4 Servings

*"A serving is one 'sandwich', but this is usually too much!
I cut them in half and let my guests decide."*
—INNKEEPER, *Rosevine Inn*

4 eggs
⅓ cup milk
1½ teaspoons cinnamon
1 tablespoon butter
4 slices multi-grain bread
2 ripe bananas, peeled and sliced lengthwise
½ cup maple syrup
Powdered sugar, for serving

In a shallow bowl, combine eggs, milk, and cinnamon; beat well. In a large skillet, melt butter over medium heat. Dip 2 pieces of bread in the egg mixture, coating each side. Place the 2 dipped slices in the skillet. Place bananas on top of the bread. Dip the remaining 2 slices of bread in the egg mixture and place on top of the slices in the skillet to make two "sandwiches." Cook on both sides until browned and cooked thoroughly.

Put French toast on warmed plates. Remove pan from heat. Pour syrup in pan for 15 seconds to warm it. Dust French toast with powdered sugar and serve with warm syrup.

BRAVA HOUSE

The Brava House is located just minutes from downtown Austin. Known for its casual and playful nature, Austin is the "playground of Texas," and the gateway to the Texas Hill Country. As the state capitol and home to the University of Texas, the city supports a politically charged and culturally rich environment. An outdoor mecca, Austin is blessed with a temperate year-round climate and 300 days of sunshine a year.

Every Sunday, the Brava House hosts a Champagne Brunch, complete with mimosas and berries with cream.

INNKEEPER:	Robin Kyle
ADDRESS:	1108 Blanco Street, Austin, Texas 78703
TELEPHONE:	(512) 478-5034 phone and fax
E-MAIL:	robin@bravahouse.com
WEBSITE:	www.bravahouse.com
ROOMS:	2 Rooms; 2 Suites; Private baths
CHILDREN:	Call ahead
PETS:	Call ahead; Resident dog

Pecan-Crusted French Toast

Makes 6 Servings

"The pecans are what make this dish stand out as a real treat!"
—INNKEEPER, *Brava House*

3 eggs
½ cup milk
2 tablespoons orange juice
1 teaspoon cinnamon
Butter, for skillet or griddle
12 slices (small in diameter) French bread
½ cup pecans, chopped
Orange slices, for garnish
Maple syrup, for serving

In a medium bowl, combine eggs, milk, orange juice, and cinnamon; beat well. In a skillet or griddle, melt butter over medium heat. Dip each piece of bread lightly in the egg mixture, coating both sides, and place on the griddle. Sprinkle and press the pecans into the uncooked side of the bread. Turn bread over to brown both sides.

Serve French toast pecan-side-up, two slices per person. Garnish each serving with a slice of orange. Serve with maple syrup on the side.

French toast is known as Eggy Bread in the United Kingdom. In Spain it is called Torrijas and is usually served during Easter.

GARDEN MANOR

"Where Dallas and Fort Worth Meet"

Asweeping veranda overlooks the tranquil grounds of the Garden Manor located in Grapevine, one of the oldest towns in Texas. Over seventy shops in Grapevine's historic shopping district are within walking distance of the inn. With the Dallas–Fort Worth Airport only seven miles from Grapevine, Garden Manor Bed and Breakfast

is a convenient resting place for the business traveler or visitor.

The décor in each guest room reflects the lovely outdoor garden. Every room has a private bath with European heated towel racks, garden-scented bath products, and two spa robes. Turndown service includes a box of fresh chocolate truffles. Early morning beverage service is provided and a full-course breakfast is served in the dining room.

The new garden room addition to the Manor has two sets of French doors that open onto the back and side lawns; a combination of indoor and outdoor space designed to accommodate events.

INNKEEPERS:	Judy and Gunther Dusek
ADDRESS:	205 East College Street, Grapevine, Texas 76051
TELEPHONE:	(817) 424-9177; (877) 424-9177
E-MAIL:	info@gardenmanorbandb.com
WEBSITE:	www.gardenmanorbandb.com
ROOMS:	3 Rooms; 1 Suite; Private baths
CHILDREN:	Ages 12 and older are welcome
PETS:	Not Allowed; Resident dog

Cinnamon French Toast

Makes 6 Servings

"Guests always want this recipe—
the buttermilk is the secret ingredient."
—INNKEEPER, *Garden Manor*

1 loaf Pepperidge Farm Brown Sugar
   and Cinnamon Bread (Thick Slice)
10 eggs
¼ cup buttermilk
¼ cup sugar
1 teaspoon pure vanilla
1 teaspoon cinnamon
½ teaspoon salt
Powdered sugar for dusting French toast
Maple syrup, for serving
2 cups of vegetable oil for frying
   (DO NOT ADD TO BATTER)

Cut each bread slice diagonally and place in large shallow pan. In a large bowl, beat eggs well; add buttermilk; fold in sugar, vanilla, cinnamon, and salt. Pour mixture over the bread slices; turning bread over after 5 minutes to coat other side. In the skillet, heat oil to medium. When oil is hot, add no more than 6 pieces of bread and cook both sides until golden brown. Drain on paper towels; sprinkle with powdered sugar while still hot. Serve with maple syrup.

HOLLY HILL
HOMESTEAD & RETREAT

"A special place with special food for special people"

The hills of northeast Texas are home to the farm-style Holly Hill Homestead and Retreat. The accommodations at the bed and breakfast are cozy, informal, and charming, and the view from the sun porch is absolutely awe-inspiring.

Country gourmet meals are prepared at Holly Hill and the food is always fresh and made from scratch. The ambiance for casual dining in the large kitchen is enhanced by the wood cook stove and open fireplace. Private dining on one of the porches or outdoors can also be arranged. New recipes are tested by the innkeeper for the regular Wednesday luncheon. It begins at noon and ends when the food runs out. Reservations are requested for the folks interested in taking part in the Wednesday taste tests.

Garden tours are offered during every season of the year at Holly Hill Homestead. Small groups may participate in gardening and cooking workshops held at the inn on a regular basis. A workshop schedule is listed on the events page of the bed and breakfast website.

INNKEEPERS: Tim and Jolene Wilson
ADDRESS: 9076 Texas Highway 11, Hughes Springs, Texas 75656
TELEPHONE: (903) 639-1318
E-MAIL: jolene@hollyhillhomestead.com
WEBSITE: www.hollyhillhomestead.com
ROOMS: 2 Rooms; Private baths
CHILDREN: Age 12 and older welcome
PETS: Not allowed

Apple French Toast with Pecans

Makes 6 Servings

4 eggs
1 cup milk
¼ cup sugar
1 teaspoon vanilla
¼ teaspoon cinnamon
Dash of salt
1 medium tart apple, peeled, cored, shredded
1 loaf French bread, cut into 1-inch slices
½ cup pecans, chopped
4 tablespoons melted butter

In a medium bowl, combine eggs and milk; beat well. Add sugar, vanilla, cinnamon, salt and apple; mix well. (Make sure you add the apple to the egg and milk mixture as soon as it is shredded. This will keep the apple from turning brown.) Set mixture aside.

Grease a 9x13-inch pan. Dip bread slices into egg mixture; arrange in pan. Use enough slices to fill pan entirely, but do not overcrowd. Pour rest of egg mixture over bread. Cover pan and refrigerate overnight.

In the morning, preheat oven to 400°F. Remove pan from the refrigerator and let set at room temperature for 30 minutes before baking. Sprinkle with pecans and drizzle with butter. Bake for 20–30 minutes or until puffed and golden. Serve with additional sautéed apples and syrup.

LET'S GO COUNTRY

You are invited to settle into the peace and privacy of country living in this renovated 1913 Victorian farmhouse situated on 127 acres of working farm near Waco. Meander along White Rock Creek and view the peaceful lakes. Walk among the Texas wildflowers

and through the quiet woods. Make time to visit with the resident Longhorns. They are lovingly referred to as "Texas Art on the Hoof." The sire of the herd, Jabez, may introduce you to the newborn calf. The markings on the calf resemble those of her mother Abigail. The calf was named Ruth but the name was changed to Babe Ruth when it was discovered that the calf was male.

After a day outdoors, take it easy, and reflect on your perfect day in the country. View the beautiful landscape from your second story window in the sitting area of the Shady Oaks Suite. Soak in the jetted claw-foot tub, and then snuggle into the king-size sleigh bed for a night as peaceful as your day.

INNKEEPERS: John and Marcia Boggs

ADDRESS: 1182 Spring Lake Road, Waco, Texas 76705
MAILING: (PO Box 154444) 76715

TELEPHONE: (254) 799-7947; (888) 239-2517; (254) 867-0362 fax

E-MAIL: info@letsgocountry.com

WEBSITE: www.letsgocountry.com

ROOMS: 4 Suites; Private baths

CHILDREN: Age 10 and older welcome

PETS: Not allowed; Resident dog

Blueberry-Cream Cheese French Toast

Makes 6 to 8 Servings

"Having been raised in blueberry country—Michigan—our family would pick pounds of blueberries every spring. We three kids would eat half of what we picked, but mom never seemed to mind. We always looked forward to her blueberry-cream cheese French toast."
—INNKEEPER, *Let's Go Country*

1 small loaf French bread
    (cut into 1-inch cubes)
2 (8-ounce) packages cream cheese,
    cut into 1-inch cubes
1½ cups fresh blueberries
12 eggs
2 cups milk
6 tablespoons maple syrup

Butter a 9x13-inch baking dish. Place half of the bread cubes in the baking dish. Place the cream cheese cubes on top of the bread cubes; distributed equally. Arrange the blueberries over the cheese cubes. Spread remaining bread cubes on top.

In a medium bowl, combine eggs, milk, and maple syrup. Pour mixture over ingredients in baking dish. Cover and refrigerate overnight.

The next morning, preheat oven to 350°F. Remove baking dish from refrigerator. If dish is glass, it should set until glass is at room temperature to avoid shattering in the oven. Bake covered for 30 minutes. Remove cover and continue baking for an additional 30 minutes. Serve with blueberry preserves or syrup.

MARIPOSA RANCH

During your days at the Mariposa Ranch, enjoy the small-town charm of Brenham and the many attractions throughout Washington County. Back at the ranch, enjoy the charming surroundings, including live oak trees, grand vistas, sumptuous breakfasts, massages, candlelight dinners, and a crackling fire in the privacy of your room or cottage.

Breakfast includes such treats as Texas Ranger baked eggs, Hill Country baked apples with lemon cream sauce, and German peach kuchen.

And it seems that the resident dogs are quite a hit with the guests. While many of the guests' comments included the canines, here are just two of them:

"We enjoyed the dogs! It's especially nice when your room comes complete with a private porch and porch dog!" —GUEST

INNKEEPERS:	Johnna & Charles Chamberlain
ADDRESS:	8904 Mariposa Lane, Brenham, Texas 77833
TELEPHONE:	(979) 836-4737; (877) 647-4774; (979) 836-2565 fax
E-MAIL:	info@mariposaranch.com
WEBSITE:	www.mariposaranch.com
ROOMS:	4 Rooms; 2 Suites; 5 Cottages; Private baths
CHILDREN:	Welcome
PETS:	Not allowed; Resident cat & dogs

Orange Pecan French Toast

Makes 4 to 6 Servings

*This is a very flavorful French toast,
and it makes a beautiful presentation.
Start the preparation for this dish the night before serving.*

4 eggs
$2/3$ cup orange juice
$1/3$ cup milk
¼ cup sugar
¼ teaspoon nutmeg
¼ teaspoon vanilla
¼ cup Triple Sec (orange-flavored liqueur)
12 (1-inch thick) slices French bread
$1/3$ cup butter, melted
2 tablespoons orange zest, grated
½ cup pecan pieces
Maple syrup, for serving

In a medium bowl, mix eggs, orange juice, milk, sugar, nutmeg, vanilla, and Triple Sec. Dip each bread slice in the egg mixture; lightly coat each side, and place in a single layer on an ungreased 10x15-inch or larger jelly-roll pan or rimmed baking sheet. If there is any remaining egg mixture, pour it over the French toast in the pan. Cover and refrigerate overnight.

Preheat oven to 400°F. Spray a baking sheet with nonstick cooking spray. Arrange soaked bread slices in a single layer on the baking sheet. Drizzle melted butter over bread slices. Sprinkle with orange zest. Top with pecan pieces. Bake for 30–40 minutes, or until golden brown. Serve with syrup.

BLUE HERON INN

Get a little taste of country while experiencing the generous spaces of the expansive Blue Heron Inn located in Cedar Creek, just ten minutes west of historic Bastrop. As you approach the four-and-a-half-acre property, you may see ducks or a blue heron visiting the large pond in front of the two-story Colonial-style home. Or, you may spot a guest who's fishing in the well-stocked pond. Fishing poles are provided by the inn.

Walk through the front door into the spacious front room with a twenty-one-foot ceiling and five eighteen-foot windows. Entrances to the four large guest bedrooms are at the top of the grand staircase.

Snacks and beverages are always available in the upstairs guest kitchen.

The New Orleans Crawfish Omelet is the morning specialty of the Blue Heron, but you may select your favorite item from the gourmet breakfast menu. After your meal, relax on the garden patio behind the home. Sit and watch the goldfish swim in the small pond and listen to the waterfall as you let your worries slip away.

INNKEEPERS: Janice and Al Mouton

ADDRESS: 583 Union Chapel Road, Cedar Creek, Texas 78612

TELEPHONE: (512) 789-9597; (512) 332-2445 fax

E-MAIL: blueheron@blueheron-bnb.com

WEBSITE: www.blueheron-bnb.com

ROOMS: 4 Rooms; Private baths

CHILDREN: Age 12 and older are welcome

PETS: Not allowed; Resident dog

Praline Sauce

Makes 6 to 10 Servings

½ cup butter
¾ cup brown sugar
¾ cup maple syrup
1 cup toasted pecans, chopped

In a saucepan, melt butter and brown sugar. Add maple syrup and pecans; heat through. Serve over pancakes and waffles.

We all have hometown appetites.

Every other person is a bundle

of longing for the simplicities of

good taste once enjoyed on the farm

or in the hometown left behind.

—CLEMENTINE PADDLEFORD

Fruit Specialties

Fruit Specialties

"*A fruit is a vegetable*
with looks and money.
Plus, if you let fruit rot,
it turns into wine, something
Brussels sprouts never do."

—P.J. O'ROURKE

LAKEHOUSE B&B

"Lakehouse Bed and Breakfast was my childhood home.
My family relocated to Canyon Lake in the late 70s
and it was here that I learned to swim, fish, and water ski.
It was after meeting my wife that we decided to pursue
our dream of owning a bed & breakfast."

—INNKEEPER

An unobstructed view of Canyon Lake can be seen from this contemporary Mediterranean-style inn near New Braunfels in the Texas Hill Country. The luxuries of a stroll along the shoreline at sunrise, an afternoon lounging next to the sparkling blue pool, or stargazing from the vine-draped hot tub are all included in the price

of the room at the Lakehouse. In the evening, slip into a spa robe and slippers, delve into a book from the inn's library and partake in a compli-mentary beverage from your guestroom's refrigerator. Modern day amenities include high-speed wireless Internet, cable television, and DVD and CD players.

Breakfast is typically served at your individual private table in the dining room overlooking the lake. Breakfast can also be enjoyed in the lakeside courtyard if the weather permits.

INNKEEPERS: Justin and Jean Robinson

ADDRESS: 1519 Glenn Drive, Canyon Lake, Texas 78133

TELEPHONE: (830) 899-5099; (866) 616-5253

E-MAIL: questions@thelakehousebb.com

WEBSITE: www.thelakehousebb.com

ROOMS: 2 Rooms; 2 Suites; 2 Cottages; Private baths

CHILDREN: Age 12 and older welcome

PETS: Not allowed

Citrus Segments in Vanilla Bean Syrup

Makes 6 Servings

"My father's favorite dish."
—INNKEEPER, *Lakehouse Bed and Breakfast*

1⅓ cups water
⅔ cups sugar
1 vanilla bean, split in half lengthwise
4 large oranges
2 large grapefruit
Mint sprigs, to garnish

In a saucepan, stir together water and sugar; add the vanilla bean; bring to a simmer over medium heat stirring frequently. Once sugar is dissolved, remove from heat and let cool. Discard the vanilla bean.

Section the oranges and grapefruit by cutting off the ends of each fruit to reveal the flesh. Carefully cut the remaining peel off by following the contour of the fruit. Cut along each segment. Gently toss the fruit segments into the syrup. Cover and refrigerate until well chilled. Serve in small bowls; garnish with mint sprigs.

Citrus trees were first planted along the Rio Grande in 1882. Now, Texas has one of the largest citrus industries in the United States.

AMERICAN HERITAGE HOUSE

This spectacular Federal-style mansion is quietly positioned in the lush Brazos River Valley in the northern Texas town of Granbury. The innkeepers at American Heritage House welcome you through the nineteenth-century doorway into a Texas Bed and Breakfast clearly beyond the ordinary. The 1,630-square-foot wrap around porch allows ample room for daydreams to take flight. A piano in the music room is available for melodious guests and a sixty-five-inch theatre screen complete with a DVD library offers the opportunity to escape and be entertained. Putters and golf balls are provided for the on-site putting green.

Each of the six boutique bedrooms and the three cottages are enchantingly unique. All guests are treated to a multi-course gourmet sit-down breakfast fit for royalty. The meal is served on fine china and crystal in the formal dining room. The American Heritage House event facility can accommodate up to sixty people and is just the right size for corporate retreats.

INNKEEPERS: Ron and Karen Bleeker

ADDRESS: 225 West Moore Street, Granbury, Texas 76048

TELEPHONE: (817) 578-3768; (866) 778-3768

E-MAIL: info@americanheritagehouse.com

WEBSITE: www.americanheritagehouse.com

ROOMS: 4 Rooms; 2 Suites; 3 Cottages

CHILDREN: Welcome in the cottages; Age 12 and older in the main house

PETS: Not allowed

Heritage House Hot Fruit Compote

Make 12 to 14 Servings

FRUIT COMPOTE:

2 cans pears, drained,
  cut into bite-size pieces
12–14 maraschino cherries
2 cans peaches, drained,
  cut into bite-size pieces
2 cans pineapple chunks
  cut into bite-size pieces

1 can apricots, drained,
  cut into bite-size pieces
3 tablespoons flour
1 cup brown sugar
1 teaspoon cinnamon
4 tablespoons butter

DEVONSHIRE CREAM:

1 cup confectioner's sugar
1 cup heavy sweet cream

1 (8-ounce) cup sour cream
1 teaspoon vanilla or almond extract

For fruit compote: Preheat oven to 325°F. Coat a 4-quart baking dish with cooking spray. Add fruit. In a small bowl, combine flour, brown sugar, and cinnamon. Sprinkle evenly over fruit. Dot with butter. Bake 1 hour. Remove from oven; allow to cool.

Remove cherries from the compote and set aside. Once cherries are removed, stir remaining fruit compote to blend topping throughout the dish. Spoon compote into individual serving dishes.

For Devonshire cream: In a medium bowl, combine sugar and cream; whisk until smooth, but shy of the consistency of whipped cream. Fold in sour cream and vanilla; continue whisking until almost smooth. Refrigerate overnight to allow the mixture to "weep." Before serving, use a spatula to drain off the accumulated liquid by holding the mixture to one side of the container and putting pressure on the cream mixture to force excess liquid to other side of bowl. Drain.

Top each fruit compote with Devonshire cream and top with a baked cherry.

TIPS:

Layer fruit in order beginning with pears on the bottom; make a pocket for the cherries; then add peaches, pineapples, and apricots. (The pears take longer to break down into soft tissue consistent with the rest of the fruit; and the cherries tend to toughen if exposed among the top layers.)

The Devonshire cream will keep up to 5 days in the refrigerator. Drain off excess liquid each time and stir to maintain proper consistency.

GREAT OAKS MANOR

Massive Corinthian columns flank the front porch steps of this three-story Sugar Land and Houston area bed and breakfast called Great Oaks Manor. Civil War hero Clement Newton Bassett incorporated resplendent period architectural details into the design when he built his stunning Greek Revival residence that now serves as an impressive inn. The majestic carved oak staircase is accented with stained-glass windows that shine into the stately foyer. There are eight fireplaces with the original wood or marble mantles, which provide authentic ambience in this mansion steeped in colorful Texas history.

The two-acre grounds where century-old oaks create a shady canopy are a natural invitation to take a nap in the old-fashioned hammock. A lavish breakfast buffet is served daily in the elegant dining room or on the verandah. Murder mystery weekends are scheduled regularly at the Great Oaks Manor and feature a pirate feast proceeding the murder and mayhem.

INNKEEPERS: Carey and Fred Gulliksen

ADDRESS: 419 Macek Road, Richmond, Texas 77469

TELEPHONE: (281) 343-9551

E-MAIL: info@greatoaksmanor.com

WEBSITE: www.GreatOaksManor.com

ROOMS: 6 Rooms; Private baths

CHILDREN: Ages 12 and older are welcome

PETS: Not allowed; Resident dogs, cats, and many chickens and ducks

Ginger Pecan Apples

Makes 8 Servings

"This is a wonderful dish to serve on cold winter mornings.
Try to use apples sweeter than a Granny Smith. If you use tart apples,
make cuts from the top, inside the skin as if you were making wedges,
but don't pierce the skin. Make about 8 cuts per apple to help
distribute the sweetness in the apples."
—INNKEEPER, *Great Oaks Manor*

8 medium baking apples, not too tart
½ cup toasted pecans, chopped
1⅓ cup brown sugar, packed
½ cup butter, preferably European style
2 teaspoons cinnamon
1 teaspoon nutmeg
¼ cup candied ginger, chopped
1 teaspoon vanilla

Preheat oven to 350°F.

Wash and core apples; do not peel. Do not core clear through the bottom. The best way to do this is to cut a thin slice off the top of the apple, then scoop out the core with a small metal melon baller. Place apples in a 9x13-inch baking dish.

In a small bowl, combine all the remaining ingredients. Spoon filling into the apples, piling extra on top to use all the filling. Bake for 30–45 minutes until apples are tender.

Serve apples warm, spooning any extra sauce drippings from the baking dish, over the apples.

Apples may also be baked in a crock-pot. Place apples on a rack in the crock-pot and add ½ cup water. Cover and cook on low for 8–10 hours.

OLD MULBERRY INN

Named for the oldest mulberry tree in Jefferson, and situated on park-like grounds, the Old Mulberry Inn is just a few doors from the home where Lady Bird Johnson lived as a teenager. The inn's extensive landscaping and splendid roses earned Jefferson's coveted "Garden of the Month" award.

The Old Mulberry Inn's well-traveled owners have created a bed and breakfast that represents the very best of the inns that they themselves have experienced here and abroad. The inn combines the look of the past with the comforts of the present, while reflecting the nineteenth-century charm of historic Jefferson.

"Personal guest attention, together with the unique charm and ambience of the property, combine to make the bed and breakfast experience one unlike any other."

—AMERICAN AUTOMOBILE ASSOCIATION (AAA)

INNKEEPERS: Donald and Gloria Degn

ADDRESS: 209 East Jefferson Street, Jefferson, Texas 75657

TELEPHONE: (903) 665-1945

E-MAIL: mulberry3@charter.net

WEBSITE: www.oldmulberryinn.com

ROOMS: 5 Rooms; Private baths

CHILDREN: Children age 15 and older welcome

PETS: Not allowed

Fresh Plum Kuchen

Makes 8 to 10 Servings

1 stick (½ cup) butter, room temperature
1 cup sugar, divided
2 eggs
¾ teaspoon almond extract
½ teaspoon vanilla extract
1 cup flour
1 teaspoon baking powder
½ teaspoon salt
4–5 large plums, sliced into wedges
    or 20 small plums, cut in half
1 teaspoon cinnamon
¼ teaspoon nutmeg
Whipped cream, for serving (optional)

Preheat oven to 400°F. Spray a 9-or10-inch pie plate or round pan with nonstick cooking spray. In a large bowl, cream together butter and ½ cup sugar. Beat in eggs, one at a time. Add almond extract and vanilla extract. In a small bowl, sift flour, baking powder, and salt; add to the butter mixture; blend well. Spread batter into pan.

Arrange plum slices, slightly overlapping, around the edge of the batter. Arrange the remaining plum slices down the center of the batter, reversing directions. If using small plum halves, arrange cut-side-down on batter.

In a separate bowl, combine remaining ½ cup of sugar, cinnamon and nutmeg; sprinkle over plums and batter. Bake for 30 minutes. Cut into wedges and serve warm. Top with whipped cream, if desired.

INGLESIDE
BED AND BREAKFAST

This pristine, two-story, brick dwelling was built in 1923 on Main Street, just a short stroll from historic downtown Brenham. Connie Hall operates the bed and breakfast in her childhood home. Her parents bought the house in 1962 when Connie was five years old. She has shared her home with travelers for the past ten years and  considers it a privilege to do so. On weekend afternoons, complimentary wine and cheese are offered to overnight guests. Warm beverages are available twenty-four hours a day at the coffee bar. Crunchy French toast and caramelized banana omelets are just two of the specialties often prepared for the daily full-country gourmet breakfast.

For a delicious diversion during your stay at the Ingleside, take a guided tour of the nearby Blue Bell Creamery production facility. Named after the native Texas bluebell wildflower, each factory tour ends with a free scoop of the ice cream of your choice. Or, make plans to stay at the Ingleside during the first weekend of April or October and attend the Texas Antique Weekend, a huge antique, craft, art, and collectible gathering just minutes away from Brenham.

INNKEEPER: Connie Hall

ADDRESS: 409 East Main Street, Brenham, Texas

TELEPHONE: (979) 251-7707; (979) 353-4016 fax

E-MAIL: connie@inglesidebb.com

WEBSITE: www.inglesidebb.com

ROOMS: 6 Rooms; 1 Suite; 5 Private baths; 1 Shared bath

CHILDREN: Age 12 and older welcome

PETS: Not allowed

Baked Bananas

Makes 8 Servings

"This is a great recipe for cold mornings—and since bananas are available all year—they are as good in the winter as in the summer."
—INNKEEPER, *Ingleside Bed and Breakfast*

¼ cup unsalted butter, melted
2 lemons
8 firm bananas
¼ cup brown sugar, packed
2 tablespoons ground cinnamon
½ teaspoon ground ginger
½ cup shredded coconut
½ cup heavy cream

Preheat oven to 325°F. Pour butter into 9x13-inch baking dish. Cut 1 lemon into 8 thinly sliced pieces. Set slices aside for garnish. Squeeze juice from remainder of the sliced lemon, and the second lemon, into the butter in baking dish. Swirl to combine.

Peel each banana gently to keep whole. Place bananas in baking dish; turning to coat with butter mixture. In a small bowl, combine brown sugar, cinnamon, and ginger; using a whisk to thoroughly blend. Using half of the sugar mixture, sprinkle the top of each banana.

Bake bananas for 8 minutes. Remove from oven and turn them over. Sprinkle each banana with remaining sugar mixture and top with coconut. Return to oven for an additional 8 minutes.

Remove bananas from baking dish; slice them in half and place both halves in an individual serving dish. Pour 1 tablespoon of cream into each dish around the sides of the bananas—avoiding the tops. Add lemon garnish and serve immediately.

Baked Pecan-Stuffed Nectarines

Makes 2 Servings

¹⁄₃ cup pecan halves (reserve 4 halves)
2½ tablespoons sugar
1 large egg yolk
2 firm, ripe nectarines
2 sprigs of mint

Preheat oven to 425°F. In a small food processor, pulse pecans until finely ground. Add 2 tablespoons sugar and egg yolk; pulse until combined. Half and pit nectarines; arrange cut-side up on a small baking sheet. Divide pecan mixture among the nectarine halves, mounding it in the center. Garnish each mound with a pecan half. Sprinkle nectarines with remaining sugar.

Bake about 10 minutes, in the middle of the oven until pecan mixture is golden. Serve 2 halves in a bowl; garnish with sprig of mint.

Fruit Ice

Makes 12 Servings

*"This recipe is great to make ahead and have on hand.
It will keep up to a month in the freezer."*
—INNKEEPER, *Ingleside*

1 can (17-ounce) apricots
1 can (17-ounce) crushed pineapple
½ cup sugar
32 ounces frozen strawberries in syrup
6 ounces frozen orange juice concentrate
2 tablespoons fresh lemon juice
3½ ripe bananas, sliced
Optional fruit: fresh nectarines,
    red or green grapes, halved
Sprigs of mint for garnish

Drain canned fruit; reserving 2 cups of liquid. In a large saucepan, combine fruit liquid and sugar; cook for 5 minutes or until sugar is dissolved. Remove saucepan from the stove. Add strawberries, frozen orange juice, and lemon juice to the syrup. Add drained apricots and pineapple. Add bananas. You may add any additional fruit up to 6 more cups.

Put mixture in a plastic container and freeze. To serve, spoon into sherbet glasses and garnish with mint.

BEAUREGARD HOUSE

The Hemingway Suite at the Mobil Three Star and AAA Three Diamond Beauregard House is decorated with Oriental silks, Egyptian carpets, and original paintings. This room takes you back to an earlier time—the furnishings are English Victorian and the room is decorated in the lavish style of early twentieth-century Europe.

While staying in this historic city, visitors have no need for a car—complimentary trolley tickets are provided to guests staying at the Beauregard.

To enhance your stay, the Beauregard offers additional special packages: Birthday cakes, balloons, gift baskets, flowers, and spa packages.

INNKEEPERS: Kenneth Mohundro and Roland Quintanilla

ADDRESS: 215 Beauregard Street, San Antonio, Texas 78204

TELEPHONE: (210) 222-1198; (888) 667-0555

E-MAIL: relax@thebeauregardhouse.com

WEBSITE: www.beauregardhouse.com

ROOMS: 3 Rooms; 3 Suites; Private baths

CHILDREN: Age 16 and older welcome

PETS: Not allowed; Resident dog

Strawberry Semifreddo

Makes 6 Servings

Semifreddo in Italian means "half cold". This recipe features toasted blueberry English muffins filled with a partially frozen, sweetened strawberry and whipped cream purée, topped with sliced strawberries and chocolate sauce. "A true culinary delight."
—INNKEEPER, *Beauregard House*

2 pints fresh strawberries, divided
3 egg whites
1 teaspoon plus 1½ teaspoons vanilla extract
⅓ cup sugar
¾ cup whipped cream
3 tablespoons powdered sugar
1 tablespoon lemon juice
6 blueberry English muffins, cut in half and toasted
6 tablespoons chocolate sauce, for garnish

Purée 1 pint of strawberries in a blender. In a medium bowl, combine strawberry purée, egg whites and 1 teaspoon of vanilla. Beat with a mixer until frothy, about 2 minutes. Gradually beat in sugar. Fold in whipped cream. Freeze mixture for 1 hour.

In a small bowl, slice remaining 1 pint of strawberries. Toss with 1½ teaspoons vanilla, powdered sugar, and lemon juice; cover and chill.

To serve, place 1 toasted English muffin bottom half on each of 6 plates. Spoon the strawberry purée mixture into the center of each muffin half. Top with the sliced strawberry mixture. Place the English muffin tops on top at an angle (so your guests can see the berries and the semifreddo). Drizzle 1 tablespoon of chocolate sauce onto each plate for garnish.

THE COOK'S COTTAGE & SUITES

Innkeeper Patsy Bynum Swendson is a nationally recognized authority on Southwestern cuisine who has delighted radio and television audiences for over 20 years, authored 49 cookbooks and has been a contributing writer for nine national magazines.

If gourmet dining is high on your list while staying at a bed and breakfast—then this is the place for you. Some of Patsy's recipes featured in other cookbooks include: Tortilla Turtles, Enchilada Suizas, Gringo Migas, and Texas Sunburst. What are these wonderful delights?

Located in the heart of the Texas Hill Country, The Cook's Cottage has been selected by *Travel and Leisure* magazine as "One of the Top 25 Most Romantic Places in the U.S."

INNKEEPER:	Patsy Swendson
ADDRESS:	703 West Austin, Fredericksburg, Texas 78624
TELEPHONE:	(210) 493-5101; (888) 991-6749; (866) 869-0364 fax
E-MAIL:	patsyswendson@yahoo.com
WEBSITE:	www.bed-inn-breakfast-tx.com
ROOMS:	3 Rooms; 2 Suites; 1 Cottage; Private baths
CHILDREN:	Unable to accommodate
PETS:	Not allowed

Melon with Black Forest Ham & Strawberry Salsa

Makes 4 Servings

"Slices of cool, fragrant cantaloupe topped with thin slices of Black Forest ham is yummy enough, but paired with ginger- and orange-scented strawberry salsa, you can't help but win! A wonderful side dish for brunch."
—INNKEEPER, *The Cook's Cottage & Suites*

CANTALOUPE AND HAM:
1 large ripe cantaloupe
6 ounces Black Forest ham, sliced into thin julienne strips

STRAWBERRY SALSA:
8 ounces strawberries, hulled and diced
1 teaspoon sugar
2 tablespoons freshly squeezed orange juice
1 teaspoon orange zest, grated
½ teaspoon fresh ginger, finely grated

For Cantaloupe and Ham: Cut cantaloupe in half and remove seeds. Cut melon halves into thick slices. Chill until ready to serve. Arrange the melon on a serving plate. Sprinkle strips of ham over the melon. Serve with strawberry salsa.

For Strawberry Salsa: Combine diced berries and sugar; crush berries slightly to release juices. Stir in orange juice, orange zest and ginger.

MURSKI HOMESTEAD

"It ain't bragging if it's a fact!"
Voted "Best Weekend Escape" by *Inn Traveler* Magazine

The Murski Homestead was the original cotton farm built in the 1880s by the great-great- grandparents of the husband of the innkeeper. Today the visitor is pampered with the amenities of luxury while enjoying the quiet simplicity of country life. Relax in the evening on the century-old front porch and listen to the sounds of wildlife.

There are three beautiful rooms to choose from all named after herbs: the Lavender Room, the Sage Room, and the Rosemary Room—all with private baths and wonderfully comfortable beds with luxurious bed linens.

The Murskis also host cooking classes. Refer to their website for an up-to-date schedule.

INNKEEPER:	Pamela Murski
ADDRESS:	1662 Old Independence Road, Brenham, Texas 77833
TELEPHONE:	(979) 830-1021; (877) 690-0676
E-MAIL:	pmurski@sbcglobal.net
WEBSITE:	www.murskihomesteadbb.com
ROOMS:	3 Rooms; Private baths
CHILDREN:	Ages 10 and older are welcome
PETS:	Not allowed; Resident cats, a dog, donkeys and Longhorns

Spiced Melon Balls

Makes 8 to 10 Servings

1 ripe cantaloupe
1 ripe honeydew melon
½ teaspoon salt
1 teaspoon ground coriander
¼ teaspoon cayenne, or to taste
1 tablespoon cilantro leaves, finely minced
2 tablespoons freshly squeezed lime juice
Sugar, to taste (optional)

Use a melon baller to remove all the flesh from the melons. In a bowl, combine the melon balls, salt, coriander, cayenne, cilantro, and lime juice. Taste and adjust seasoning. If the melon is not sufficiently sweet, add a bit of sugar. Cover and refrigerate until ready to serve. It is best if eaten within 2 hours.

BLUE HERON INN

Get a little taste of country while experiencing the generous spaces of the expansive Blue Heron Inn located in Cedar Creek, just ten minutes west of historic Bastrop. As you approach the four-and-a-half-acre property, you may see ducks or a blue heron visiting the large pond in front of the two-story Colonial-style home. Or, you may spot a guest who's fishing in the well-stocked pond. Fishing poles are provided by the inn.

Walk through the front door into the spacious front room with a twenty-one-foot ceiling and five eighteen-foot windows. Entrances to the four large guest bedrooms are at the top of the grand staircase.

Snacks and beverages are always available in the upstairs guest kitchen.

The New Orleans Crawfish Omelet is the morning specialty of the Blue Heron, but you may select your favorite item from the gourmet breakfast menu. After your meal, relax on the garden patio behind the home. Sit and watch the goldfish swim in the small pond and listen to the waterfall as you let your worries slip away.

INNKEEPERS:	Janice and Al Mouton
ADDRESS:	583 Union Chapel Road, Cedar Creek, Texas 78612
TELEPHONE:	(512) 789-9597; (512) 332-2445 fax
E-MAIL:	blueheron@blueheron-bnb.com
WEBSITE:	www.blueheron-bnb.com
ROOMS:	4 Rooms; Private baths
CHILDREN:	Age 12 and older are welcome
PETS:	Not allowed; Resident dog

Fruit Topping

Makes 4 to 6 Servings

4 ounces cream cheese, softened
2 (8-ounce) containers vanilla yogurt
⅓ cup brown sugar
½ teaspoon cinnamon

Using electric mixer, mix cream cheese, yogurt, brown sugar, and cinnamon until smooth. Use as a topping on fresh fruit.

Live each season as it passes;

breathe the air, drink the drink,

taste the fruit, and resign yourself

to the influences of each.

—HENRY DAVID THOREAU

BEAUMONT RANCH

Beaumont Ranch

The Beaumont Ranch, located 30 minutes south of Dallas and Fort Worth, is "extravagantly Texan." The Old Chisholm Trail runs right through the middle of the ranch, which is not a dude-wrangling operation but a working ranch with 2000 head of cattle, horse-breeding stock and a dozen full-time ranch hands.

At the Beaumont Ranch, trail rides are true to the spirit of Texas. With seven miles of ranch roads and hilly landscapes with beautiful vistas, each ride is an experience you will cherish and enjoy. The horses are hand-selected and trained on the ranch with enough spirit to provide a real riding experience but gentle enough for beginners.

"Come join us and share in the 'Spirit of Texas'—from cowboys to cattle barons." —INNKEEPERS

INNKEEPERS: Ron and Linda Beaumont
ADDRESS: 10736 County Road 102, Grandview, Texas 76050
TELEPHONE: (817) 866 4867; (888) 864-6935; (817) 866 4453 fax
E-MAIL: information@beaumontranch.com
WEBSITE: www.beaumontranch.com
ROOMS: 16 Rooms; Private & shared baths
CHILDREN: Welcome
PETS: Not allowed; Resident horses & cats

Marshmallow Dip for Fruit

Makes 10 to 12 Servings

*For a beautiful presentation, surround the dip with
an assortment of colorful, seasonal fresh fruit on a silver tray.
Some fruits to consider: pineapple chunks, green and
purple grapes, strawberries, thick banana slices, kiwi chunks,
seedless orange segments, tart apple slices, and mango cubes.
Be sure to offer toothpicks for ease of spearing and eating.*

1 (8-ounce) package cream cheese, room temperature
1 (14-ounce) jar marshmallow crème (marshmallow fluff)

In a medium bowl, combine softened cream cheese and marsh-mallow crème. Beat on low speed with a mixer until smooth and well combined. Cover and chill until ready to serve.

Tip:
To help prevent sticking, spray a rubber spatula lightly with nonstick cooking spray before removing marshmallow crème from the jar.

Side Dishes

Side Dishes

> " *Oil and potatoes*
> *both grow underground—*
> *so French fries may have*
> *eventually produced themselves,*
> *had they not been invented.* "
>
> —J. ESTHER

LittleGoose LakeHaus

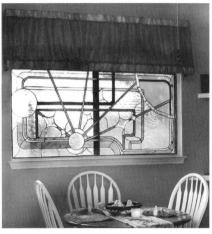

Pause to appreciate the whimsical, pink concrete couch at the entrance to the private front yard of the Little-Goose LakeHaus. Continue toward the inn through the natural landscaping of the private front yard, up the little hill, and through the gate of the wooden picket fence and you will find this eclectic, original, small, and cozy bed and breakfast.

The inn is perched on the south side of Canyon Lake near the Texas Hill Country town of Startzville. There is ample parking for guests, even if you bring a boat.

Lodge in a romantic mini-suite that includes the Gander Room with a dreamy, warm fireplace corner and a king-size bed with an artistic headboard fashioned out of copper pipe and intertwining vines. There is a secluded hot tub just outside of the Gander Room. The adjoining Breakfast Room has a lovely stained-glass window and a view of the yard and lake. A deck extends this room into the out-of-doors.

Comal Park is just down the hill and around the corner from LittleGoose Lakehaus. A nice swimming area and an offshore island are yours to explore in the park.

INNKEEPER:	Sherry Gansle
ADDRESS:	1100 Hillcrest Forest, Canyon Lake, Texas 78133
TELEPHONE:	(830) 899-3828; (866) 834-8160; (830) 899-5580 fax
E-MAIL:	desk@littlegooselakehaus.com
WEBSITE:	www.littlegooselakehaus.com
ROOMS:	1 Suite; Private bath
CHILDREN:	Welcome
PETS:	Not allowed

Sausage and Apple Braid

Makes 6 to 8 Servings

½ (17 1¼-ounce) package of frozen puff pastry
  (one sheet)
10 ounces pork sausage
  (Jimmy Dean sage or maple flavor)
2 eggs, beaten (divided use)
1 onion, finely chopped
2 apples, finely chopped
¾ cup dried herb stuffing mix
Beaten egg to glaze
1 tablespoon sesame seeds
Apple slices and sage leaves to garnish (optional)

Preheat oven to 400°F. Roll out pastry on to a 18x14-inch baking sheet. In a large bowl, mix sausage, one beaten egg, onion, apples, and stuffing mix. Spoon sausage filling down center of pastry, leaving about 2½-inches of pastry at top and bottom and 4-inches on each side of filling. Brush edges of pastry with beaten egg and fold top and bottom (on long side) over filling.

Make 3-inch cuts at ½-inch intervals down each side of pastry. Fold one strip over filling from alternate sides until filling is completely enclosed. Brush with the second beaten egg and sprinkle with sesame seeds. Bake for 30 minutes, until golden. (We test the interior temperature with a thermometer to make sure it has reached 165°F.)

Serve hot or cold, garnished with apple slices and sage leaves, if desired.

A YELLOW ROSE

Staying at A Yellow Rose is as comfortable as staying with good friends—except the innkeepers place Godiva chocolates on your pillow and serve a wonderful breakfast in your room. Deb and Kit Walker strive to provide guests with the same quality and comforts that they appreciate when they are traveling.

If business brings you to stay at A Yellow Rose, all the modern communication conveniences are available in your room—free WIFI, Premium Cable TV—even a cell phone if you forgot yours.

"The wonderful breakfast just added to the beauty and perfection of a night I will remember forever." —GUEST

INNKEEPERS: Deb and Kit Walker
ADDRESS: 229 Madison, San Antonio, Texas 78204
TELEPHONE: (210) 229-9903; (800) 950-9903
E-MAIL: yellowrose@ddc.net
WEBSITE: www.ayellowrose.com
ROOMS: 5 Rooms; 1 Suite; Private baths
CHILDREN: Age 12 and older welcome
PETS: Not allowed

Sausage Puffs

Makes 4 Servings

You can also create your own delicious stuffings for these puffs. Try scrambled eggs with cooked crumbled bacon or a mixture of chopped artichoke hearts and cream cheese.

1 (10-ounce) can refrigerated
  croissant dough, unbaked
8 ounces breakfast sausage
5 tablespoons cream cheese
1 egg white
2 tablespoons sesame seeds

Preheat oven to 350°F. In a medium skillet, cook sausage until cooked through; drain any grease. Add cream cheese while the sausage is still warm; stir until completely combined.

Spread ½ of the croissant pieces on a greased baking sheet. Spoon sausage mixture over the croissant. Cover with the remaining croissant pieces; crimp the dough edges together to seal. With a pastry brush, lightly brush egg white over the top of the dough. Sprinkle with sesame seeds. Bake for 12–15 minutes. Serve warm.

AMERICAN HERITAGE HOUSE

This spectacular Federal-style mansion is quietly positioned in the lush Brazos River Valley in the northern Texas town of Granbury. The innkeepers at American Heritage House welcome you through the nineteenth-century doorway into a Texas Bed and Breakfast clearly beyond the ordinary. The 1,630-square-foot wrap around porch allows ample room for daydreams to take flight. A piano in the music room is available for melodious guests and a sixty-five-inch theatre screen complete with a DVD library offers the opportunity to escape and be entertained. Putters and golf balls are provided for the on-site putting green.

Each of the six boutique bedrooms and the three cottages are enchantingly unique. All guests are treated to a multi-course gourmet sit-down breakfast fit for royalty. The meal is served on fine china and crystal in the formal dining room. The American Heritage House event facility can accommodate up to sixty people and is just the right size for corporate retreats.

INNKEEPERS: Ron and Karen Bleeker
ADDRESS: 225 West Moore Street, Granbury, Texas 76048
TELEPHONE: (817) 578-3768; (866) 778-3768
E-MAIL: info@americanheritagehouse.com
WEBSITE: www.americanheritagehouse.com
ROOMS: 4 Rooms; 2 Suites; 3 Cottages
CHILDREN: Welcome in the cottages; Age 12 and older in the main house
PETS: Not allowed

Southern Pecan-Crusted Bacon

Makes 4 Servings

¼ cup brown sugar
8 strips thick-slice bacon
¼ cup pecans, finely chopped

Preheat oven to 400°. Coat both sides of bacon with brown sugar and lightly sprinkle top side with pecans. Place on a baking sheet; bake for 16–18 minutes. Closely watch bacon while baking. It can change from a perfect golden brown to burnt in a matter of seconds.

Use a spatula to lift onto a wire rack. Put paper toweling under the rack to catch excess drippings. Lay strips criss-cross on plate as side dish.

AMELIA'S PLACE

In an old factory building constructed in 1924, Amelia's apartment on the third floor is the only existing apartment in downtown Dallas from the 1920s.

Amelia, a feminist from Louisiana who is said to be the best cook in three parishes, offers genuine Southern hospitality. Guests say that her breakfast is so delicious and so big, you can skip lunch. Amelia also offers a very generous Happy Hour. Books and games galore provide evening entertainment along with a few tunes on a baby grand.

Guests of all persuasions are welcome. Leave your prejudices at the door.

INNKEEPER:	Amelia Core Jenkins
ADDRESS:	5425 Gaston Avenue, #112, Dallas, Texas 75214
TELEPHONE:	(214) 827-3779
E-MAIL:	ameliacorej@sbcglobal.net
WEBSITE:	www.ameliasplace.com
ROOMS:	1 Room; Private bath
CHILDREN:	Age 14 and older welcome
PETS:	Not allowed

Buttermilk Biscuits with Tomato Gravy and Bacon

Makes 5 Servings

BISCUITS:
2 cups self-rising flour
1 cup buttermilk
    (or enough to make a stiff dough)
Vegetable oil
    (enough to cover bottom of pan generously)

TOMATO GRAVY & BACON:
1 pound bacon
2–3 tablespoons all-purpose flour
1 small onion, finely chopped
1 (14½-ounce) can diced peeled tomatoes
Salt and pepper, to taste

For the biscuits: Preheat oven to 450°F. Put self-rising flour in a bowl. Add enough buttermilk to make a stiff dough. Turn dough out onto a floured surface. With floured hands, knead dough for no longer than 10 seconds. Pinch off 10 biscuit-size pieces of dough and form into round shapes (or roll dough out to ¾-inch thick and cut with a biscuit cutter.)

Pour enough oil into an 8-inch round baking pan to generously cover the bottom. Lay each biscuit in the oil; turn over so both sides are coated. When all biscuits are in the pan, pat biscuits down until sides are touching. Bake for 15 minutes on the top rack of the oven, or until biscuits are golden brown. Serve with tomato gravy or with butter and jelly or molasses.

For the tomato gravy and bacon: Fry bacon in a heavy skillet; drain on paper towels. Pour off grease, reserving 3 tablespoons of bacon grease in the skillet. Add the all-purpose flour; cook, stirring or whisking constantly, until mixture turns a deep chocolate brown. Add the onion; cook over low heat until transparent. Stir in the tomatoes and about 1 cup of water. Season with salt and pepper. Simmer until the gravy reaches the desired consistency. To serve, place hot, split biscuits on plates. Ladle tomato gravy over the biscuits. Serve with the bacon on the sides.

CHRISTMAS HOUSE

The Christmas House Bed & Breakfast is located in San Antonio, near the Alamo and the River Walk. Guests are invited to come enjoy the city that boasts of beautiful views, historic architecture, a bustling riverfront and carefully manicured parks.

The Santa Claus Room is decorated with red and white accents and is furnished with an 1880, inlaid rosewood queen-size bed with an armoire and a private veranda.

Although built in 1908, guests will find modern amenities and will enjoy a festive atmosphere year-round. The house is filled with beautiful ornaments, angels, antiques, and handmade quilts.

INNKEEPERS:	Penny and Grant Estes
ADDRESS:	2307 McCullough, San Antonio, Texas 78212
TELEPHONE:	(210) 737-2786; (800) 268-4187; (210) 734-5712
E-MAIL:	christmashsb@earthlink.net
WEBSITE:	www.christmashousebnb.com
ROOMS:	4 Rooms; 1 Suite; Private baths
CHILDREN:	Welcome
PETS:	Not allowed; Resident cat

Christmas House Hash Brown Bake

Makes 4 to 6 Servings

"This dish may be assembled the night before, omitting the egg mixture. In the morning, let the dish stand at room temperature for 30 minutes, then add the egg mixture and bake as directed. Other ingredients can be added or substituted, such as chicken, turkey, sausage, pimentos, etc. Leftovers are great for dinner!"
—INNKEEPER, *Christmas House Bed & Breakfast*

3 cups frozen shredded potatoes, thawed
1 stick (½cup) butter, melted
1 cup cooked ham, finely chopped
1 cup (4 ounces) cheese of choice, grated
¼ cup green bell pepper, finely chopped
1 (6-ounce) can mushroom pieces
Chopped onion, to taste
2 large eggs, beaten
½ cup milk
½ teaspoon salt
¼ teaspoon pepper

Preheat oven to 425°F. Put thawed potatoes between paper towels; press to remove excess moisture. Spread potatoes into an ungreased 9-inch pie pan, pressing them onto the bottom and up the sides of the pan to form a shell. Drizzle melted butter evenly over the potatoes. Bake for 25 minutes, or until slightly browned. Cool on a wire rack.

Lower oven temperature to 350°F. In a medium bowl, combine ham, cheese, green pepper, mushrooms and onions. Spoon mixture into the cooled potato shell. In a small bowl, combine eggs, milk, salt and pepper; beat well using a fork or a whisk. Pour over the ingredients in the pan. Bake for 25–30 minutes, or until set. Let stand for 10 minutes before serving.

KNITTEL HOMESTEAD INN

In Burton, halfway between Houston and Austin, sits the meticulously restored and updated Knittel Homestead Inn. Lodging is provided in The Washington House, a 1914 farmhouse, and the 1870 Knittel House, a two-story Texas Victorian built to look like a Mississippi river boat. The rooms are large and well decorated with

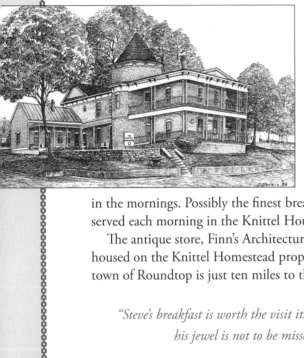

early twentieth-century antiques. Each room has a private bath, a writing desk, a sitting area, individual climate control, a television, and a clock radio.

Complementary snacks and soft drinks are available anytime in the parlor. Fresh, hot coffee and the local newspaper await you in the mornings. Possibly the finest breakfast you've ever eaten is served each morning in the Knittel House dining room.

The antique store, Finn's Architectural and Eclectic Antiques, is housed on the Knittel Homestead property, and the antique lover's town of Roundtop is just ten miles to the west of the inn.

"Steve's breakfast is worth the visit itself—what a masterpiece!! his jewel is not to be missed!" —Guest

INNKEEPERS: Steve and Carmen Finn

ADDRESS: 520 North Main Street, Burton, Texas 77835

MAILING: (PO Box 84) 77835

TELEPHONE: (979) 289-5102; (979) 289-0067

E-MAIL: stay@knittelhomestead.com

WEBSITE: www.knittelhomestead.com

ROOMS: 6 Rooms; Private baths

CHILDREN: Age 12 and older welcome

PETS: Not allowed; Resident dog

Knittel Homestead Cottage Potatoes

Makes 6 Servings

"This original recipe is our guests' favorite!"
—INNKEEPER, *Knittel Homestead Inn*

12–18 small red potatoes
6–8 tablespoons canola oil
1 yellow onion; halved and
    sliced into strips (not rings)
½ red bell pepper, julienne
Kosher salt and black pepper, to taste
¾ cup brown sugar, packed

Cut unpeeled potatoes into quarters, boil in salted water until fork tender. Drain thoroughly. In a 12-inch iron skillet, heat canola oil; when hot, carefully add potatoes to skillet. Brown potatoes, turning to brown on all sides. When potatoes are about halfway browned, add onion; cook until onions are soft and opaque. Add red pepper toward the end of the browning stage. Cook just until red peppers soften.

Salt and pepper to taste.

Sprinkle brown evenly over potato mixture. Continue cooking until brown sugar begins to caramelize and creates an even glaze. Serve immediately.

BEAUMONT RANCH

The Beaumont Ranch is much more than its lodging—although with 16 different rooms to choose from, you are sure to find the perfect fit. It is even more than its 3,200 acres of beautiful rolling hills, ponds and wildlife.

The ranch is renowned for its full-service spa, Beau-Monde Spa. Many guests have made it an integral part of time spent while at the ranch. The spa uses the newest treatments available, including the popular hot rock massage and micro-dermabrasion.

And let's not forget weddings—at Beaumont Ranch, Texas style means independence and individuality, and this is translated into each Beaumont Ranch wedding.

INNKEEPERS: Ron and Linda Beaumont
ADDRESS: 10736 County Road 102, Grandview, Texas 76050
TELEPHONE: (817) 866-4867; (888) 864-6935; (817) 866-4453 fax
E-MAIL: information@beaumontranch.com
WEBSITE: www.beaumontranch.com
ROOMS: 16 Rooms; Private & shared baths
CHILDREN: Welcome
PETS: Not allowed; Resident horses & cats

Hash Brown Casserole

Makes 10 Servings

1 (30-ounce) bag frozen
   shredded hash brown potatoes
1 small yellow onion, chopped
1 stick (½ cup) butter, melted
8 ounces Velveeta cheese, melted
1 cup sour cream
1 (10-ounce) can cream of chicken soup

TOPPING:
1½ cups crushed corn flakes
½ stick (¼ cup) butter, melted

Preheat oven to 325°F. Put frozen potatoes and chopped onions in an ungreased 9x13-inch baking dish. Pour ¼ cup melted butter over the potatoes and onions. In a separate bowl, combine melted Velveeta, sour cream, and soup; pour over the ingredients in the baking dish.

Top with crushed corn flakes. Drizzle remaining ¼ cup melted butter over the corn flakes. Bake, uncovered, for 45–60 minutes (the longer it bakes, the crispier the top).

NOTE:
This dish can be prepared a day ahead (except for the corn flakes and butter topping); covered and refrigerated. Top with the corn flakes and ½ stick of melted butter just before baking.

GEORGE BLUCHER HOUSE

Breakfast at the George Blucher House is quite an affair. Guests have compared it to an elegant dinner party. Served by candlelight in the inn's beautiful dining room, often on the innkeeper's great-grandmother's china, with sterling silver flatware, crystal stemware, and exquisite linens, the inn's breakfasts are multi-course gourmet delights.

During late fall and early spring, breakfast may be served outdoors on the back veranda where guests dine bistro-style on white, French wrought iron tables and chairs overlooking the koi pond with fountain.

"One of the best bed and breakfasts in Texas."
—*FROMMER'S TEXAS* 2001

INNKEEPER:	Tracey Love Smith
ADDRESS:	211 North Carrizo, Corpus Christi, Texas 78401
TELEPHONE:	(361) 884-4884; (866) 884-4884; (361) 884-4885 fax
E-MAIL:	blucherhousebnb@sbcglobal.net
WEBSITE:	www.georgeblucherhouse.com
ROOMS:	5 Rooms; 1 Suite; Private baths
CHILDREN:	Call ahead
PETS:	Not allowed; Resident dog & cat

Oven-Roasted New Potatoes with Prosciutto & Rosemary

Makes 8 to 10 Servings

NOTE: *The recipe may be cut in half and baked in a 7x11-inch baking dish. The baking time and temperature remain the same.*

6 pounds new potatoes, washed and scrubbed
1 stick (½ cup) butter, room temperature
6 ounces prosciutto, coarsely chopped
¼ cup extra-virgin olive oil
8 sprigs fresh rosemary (leaves only), snipped or chopped,
    plus additional rosemary sprigs, for garnish
1 teaspoon coarse sea salt
½ teaspoon freshly ground pepper

In a large deep pot, boil potatoes for 15–20 minutes until potatoes are still a bit firm when pierced with a fork. (Do not overcook.) Drain potatoes and let cool enough to handle.

Preheat oven to 450°F. While potatoes are cooling, coat sides and bottom of a 9x13-inch baking dish with butter. (It will seem like too much, but use it all—it's delicious!) In a large bowl, combine prosciutto, olive oil, rosemary, sea salt and pepper. Coarsely chop warm potatoes; add them to the ingredients in the bowl and toss gently to mix. Spoon potato mixture into baking dish. Bake for 1–1½ hours, stirring about every 15 minutes, until all of the butter and oil are absorbed and the potatoes are very crisp (add more olive oil if the potatoes seem too dry). Adjust seasonings, if necessary. Serve warm, garnished with rosemary sprigs.

TIME-SAVE TIP:
Prepare the roasted potatoes a day ahead. Cool, cover and refrigerate. Bring to room temperature before re-crisping at 400°F for about 20–30 minutes, or until crisp and hot.

LEFTOVER TIP:
Add enough mayonnaise to moisten cold leftover potatoes to make a delicious and unique potato salad.

COST-CUTTER TIP:
Use chopped smoked bacon instead of prosciutto.

THE INN AT CRAIG PLACE

The Inn at Craig Place Bed & Breakfast welcomes you to the exciting, colorful and historic city of San Antonio. This stately home was built in 1891, and is listed on the National Historic Registry as part of the historic Monte Vista neighborhood. The inn is only minutes from San Antonio attractions including the Alamo, the San Antonio River Walk, and Fort Sam Houston.

Wrap-around twin porches invite you to enter the lovely house where you can relax in pampered contentment.

In the morning, the aroma of brewing coffee and the fragrance of fresh baked goods beckon you from your nest of feather pillows and down blankets.

INNKEEPERS: Gregg and Kelly Alba

ADDRESS: 117 West Craig Place, San Antonio, Texas 78212

TELEPHONE: (210) 736-1017; (877) 427-2447; (210) 737-1562

E-MAIL: stay@craigplace.com

WEBSITE: www.craigplace.com

ROOMS: 3 Rooms; 1 Suite; Private baths

CHILDREN: Age 12 and older welcome

PETS: Not allowed; Resident cat

Sweet Potato Salad

Makes 8 Servings

This delicious, unusual warm salad takes only minutes to put together if some of the preparation is done in advance. Try cooking the bacon and sweet potatoes ahead of time, as well as chopping the scallions and toasting the pecans— you'll be a relaxed host or hostess when serving.

1 (12-ounce) package bacon
½ bunch scallions (green onions), chopped
¼ cup apple cider vinegar
⅓ cup maple syrup, or more to taste
¼ cup dried cranberries or Craisins
2 pounds sweet potatoes, peeled,
    cubed and cooked (about 3 cups)
½ bunch parsley, chopped (more or less, to taste)
½ cup toasted pecans

Cook and crumble the bacon (reserve 1 tablespoon of bacon grease). In a large skillet, heat the reserved 1 tablespoon of bacon grease; add scallions and cook for 2 minutes, or until soft. Deglaze pan with vinegar and cook until liquid is reduced by half. Add maple syrup; cook for 2 minutes more. Stir in dried cranberries and bacon. Add cubed sweet potatoes and parsley; stir to combine. Serve warm or at room temperature. Garnish with toasted pecans just before serving.

SEVEN GABLES

*"Make way for a new kind of Christian retreat.
Experience God in our small town and quiet setting."* —INNKEEPER

A stay at Seven Gables will provide you the opportunity to enjoy your morning on the wrap around porch as the sun comes up. There you will find a peaceful swing and comfy porch furniture, while sipping your first cup of freshly brewed gourmet coffee.

Delight in tastefully decorated rooms with carefully selected and placed accessories. An array of bath and body products are provided for your pleasure, along with thick, fluffy towels and monogrammed robes. Dessert is served in the evening, if you aren't out taking in the sights.

If you require directions to restaurants or area attractions, you can count on your hostess to provide guidance for endless hours of enjoyment in Mount Vernon. While visiting, browse our antique, gift, and retail shops in town for the perfect item to remember your stay.

INNKEEPER:	Debi Renner
ADDRESS:	318 South Kaufman Street, Mt Vernon, Texas 75457
TELEPHONE:	(903) 537-3391
E-MAIL:	TheInnkeeperBB@aol.com
WEBSITE:	www.mtvernontexas.com
ROOMS:	1 Room; 1 Suite; Private baths
CHILDREN:	Age 13 and older welcome
PETS:	Not allowed; Resident cat and dog

Ham-and-Cheese-Stuffing Casserole

Makes 4 to 6 Servings

5 eggs

1 cup milk

½ cup sour cream

½ teaspoon garlic powder

1 (10-ounce) package frozen broccoli,
    chopped and drained

1 package stuffing mix for chicken
    (Stove Top® works well)

9 ounces (1¼ cup) ham, chopped

1 cup cheddar cheese, grated (divided)

Preheat oven to 350°F. Grease a 2-quart baking dish.

In a large bowl, combine eggs, milk, sour cream, and garlic powder; beat well. Add broccoli, dry stuffing mix, ham, and ½ cup cheese; mix lightly. Pour mixture into prepared baking dish; cover loosely with foil. Bake 1 hour. Uncover; sprinkle with remaining cheese. Bake 5 more minutes to melt the cheese.

Cheese—

milk's leap toward

immortality.

—CLIFTON FADIMAN

THE TEXAS WHITE HOUSE

Families staying at the Texas White House Bed & Breakfast will love the nearby zoo, the Log Cabin Village, Trinity Park, the Omni Theater and the Water Gardens. Romantic couples will find fine restaurants, privacy and relaxation. The inn boasts Jacuzzi tubs, a sauna, luxurious beds and a breakfast "fit for visiting royalty." Complmentary snacks and early coffee service to your room are available.

The Land of Contrast Room features a sitting area, wicker furniture, and a Texas king-size bath with claw-foot tub and shower.

The Longhorn Suite features rustic furniture, a leather recliner, a living room with fireplace, queen-size bed with sitting area, and a two-person Jacuzzi tub.

INNKEEPERS: Jamie and Grover McMains
ADDRESS: 1417 Eighth Avenue, Fort Worth, Texas 76104
TELEPHONE: (817) 923-3597; (800) 279-6491; (817) 923-0410 fax
E-MAIL: stay@texaswhitehouse.com
WEBSITE: www.texaswhitehouse.com
ROOMS: 3 Rooms; 2 Suites; Private baths
CHILDREN: Welcome
PETS: Call ahead

Green Bean Bundles

Makes 4 to 6 Servings

Great as a side dish for pot roast or baked turkey.

2 (14½-ounce) cans whole green beans, drained
6 slices uncooked bacon, each slice cut into fourths
⅓ cup packed brown sugar
1 stick (½ cup) butter
⅛ teaspoon minced garlic

Preheat oven to 350°F. Wrap 4 or 5 beans in ¼ slice of bacon, making 24 bundles (there is no need for toothpicks—the bacon sticks to itself.) Arrange bundles in an ungreased 7x11-inch baking pan.

In a saucepan, combine brown sugar, butter and garlic; bring to a boil and stir until well mixed. Pour over the green bean bundles.

Bake, uncovered, for 20 minutes. Cover the pan with foil and bake for 30 minutes more.

CHASKA HOUSE

Waxahachie is located in the north Texas prairies and lakes region thirty minutes south of Dallas. Just a short stroll from historic Waxahachie's town square, Chaska House Lodging Properties provide premier bed and breakfast accommodations, guest cottages, corporate lodging, and a classic wedding and reception site on three historic properties.

Built in 1900, The Chaska House Bed & Breakfast is a two-story frame home with twenty-one Ionic columns. This recently renovated National Register-listed home offers guestrooms and suites reflecting the lifestyles and works of well-known authors including Samuel Clemens, F. Scott Fitzgerald, Margaret Mitchell, and William Shakespeare. Ernest Hemingway is personified a few steps away in Hemingway's Retreat. Overlooking a lush tropical courtyard, two private cottages have been designed in the style of Hemingway's Key West home.

INNKEEPERS: Louis and Linda Brown

ADDRESS: 716 West Main Street, Waxahachie, Texas 75165

TELEPHONE: (972) 937-3390; (800) 931-3390; (972) 937-1780 fax

E-MAIL: chaskabb@sbcglobal

WEBSITE: www.chaskabb.com

ROOMS: 5 Rooms; 2 Cottages; Private baths, 2 shared

CHILDREN: Age 12 and older welcome

PETS: Not allowed

Perline's Baked Tomatoes

Makes 12 Servings

*"This recipe was passed down from
pre-civil war generations in the family
of a wonderful cook at a country club
in Birmingham, Alabama."*
—INNKEEPER, *The Chaska House*

10 slices of bread, cubed
1 small onion, diced
1 cup sugar
1 teaspoon red pepper
½ teaspoon salt
1 stick of butter, melted, divided
½ teaspoon salt
4 (12-ounce) cans diced tomatoes, drained

Preheat oven to 350°F. Grease a large 4-quart, 15x10-inch casserole dish.

In a large bowl, combine bread slices, onion, sugar, pepper, and salt; mix lightly. Drizzle about ¾ of the butter evenly over the dry ingredients; mix thoroughly. Add tomatoes. Pour into prepared casserole; drizzle with remaining butter. Bake 45–50 minutes.

*It's difficult to think
anything but pleasant thoughts
while eating a
homegrown tomato.*

—LEWIS GRIZZARD

Appetizers & Beverages

Appetizers & Beverages

"Men are like a fine wine.
They all start out like grapes,
and it's our job to stomp on them
and keep them in the dark
until they mature into something
you'd like to have dinner with."

—KATHLEEN MIFSUD

ROCKIN RIVER INN

The Lowrance family built their Spanish-style home in 1882 on a high bluff overlooking the Guadalupe River. Legend has it that they chose a sturdy stone structure that would protect them from the Indian attacks that had taken their first two log houses at the same location. The expansion done in 1900 was meant to make the home the finest in eastern Kerr County, and it was. With 4,000 square feet of living space, and 1,000 square feet of covered arched porches, it remains one of the Hill Country's finest historic homes.

INNKEEPER:	Ken Wardlaw
ADDRESS:	103 Skyline Road, Center Point, Texas 78010
TELEPHONE:	(830) 634-7043; (866) 424-0576
E-MAIL:	relax@rockinriverinn.com
WEBSITE:	www.rockinriverinn.com
ROOMS:	3 Rooms; 1 Suite; Private baths
CHILDREN:	Welcome
PETS:	Not allowed; Resident dog

Betty's Apple Salsa Dip

Makes 4½ Cups (enough for a group of 30 or more)

Start this recipe about 2 weeks in advance so you have plenty of time to make the candied jalapeños – a very simple process.

2 cups sour cream
1 (8-ounce) package Neufchâtel cheese, room temperature
½ teaspoon salt
1½ tablespoons apple cider vinegar
½ cup apple jelly
1 tart apple (such as Granny Smith), finely chopped
²⁄₃ cup candied jalapeños, finely chopped (recipe follows)
Apple slices and/or tortilla chips, for serving

In a medium bowl, beat sour cream and Neufchâtel cheese on high speed until creamy. Add salt, vinegar and jelly. Beat until smooth. Stir in chopped apple and candied jalapeños.

Chill for at least 1 hour before serving. (This dip may be made in advance and will keep in the refrigerator for several days.) Serve with apple slices and/or tortilla chips.

CANDIED JALAPEÑOS:
1 (12-ounce) jar pickled jalapeños
Sugar, enough to fill jar of pickled jalapeños 3 times

Drain the liquid from the jar of pickled jalapeños, leaving the peppers in the jar. Fill the jar with sugar. Put the lid on and let the peppers stand at room temperature until the sugar turns to syrup (this can take a few days). Drain the liquid and refill the jar with sugar. Let stand again, covered, until a syrup is formed. Drain liquid again and refill with sugar. Let stand again, covered, until a syrup is formed. When the sugar turns to syrup for the third time, the peppers are candied (sometimes the last sugar addition takes longer to turn to syrup; if this happens, add a few drops of vinegar or water to help the process along). Drain the peppers and they are ready to use.

THE GARDEN INN

Try to imagine living in a tropical setting in an elegant Victorian home on the balmy Texas Gulf Coast. Owners and innkeepers, Pam and Mike Gilbert have done just that for 30 years, and they enjoy sharing it with others. The exterior grounds are as beautiful as the interior. The gardens reflect the owner's love of native plants, birds, and butterflies.

Nestled among palm and oak trees in the heart of the residential area of the East End Historical District on lovely Galveston Island, the Garden Inn is ideally located near the Seawall, the Historic Strand, and the Post Office Street shopping and entertainment districts.

Having lived in the neighborhood for 30 years, Pam and Mike know all the best places to dine and can arrange for reservations, theater tickets, and carriage rides.

INNKEEPERS: Pam and Mike Gilbert

ADDRESS: 1601 Ball (Avenue H), Galveston, Texas 77550

TELEPHONE: (409) 770-0592; (888) 770-7298

E-MAIL: thegardeninn1601@aol.com

WEBSITE: www.galveston. com/gardeninn

ROOMS: 2 Rooms; 1 Suite; Private baths

CHILDREN: Age 12 and older welcome

PETS: Not allowed

Curry Dip

Makes 1½ Cups

"This dip is very popular at brunches and cocktail parties."
—INNKEEPER, *The Garden Inn*

1 cup mayonnaise
  (do not use low-fat or salad dressing)
3 tablespoons ketchup
1 tablespoon Worcestershire sauce
1 teaspoon curry powder
1 teaspoon onion juice*
Hot sauce (such as Tabasco),
  a few drops, or to taste
Salt and pepper, to taste
Raw vegetables of choice,
  crackers, chips or pita bread for serving

In a medium bowl, combine mayonnaise, ketchup, Worcestershire sauce, curry powder, onion juice, hot sauce, salt and pepper; stir until smooth. Cover and refrigerate. For full flavor development, chill for 2–3 hours before serving. Serve with your choice of fresh raw vegetables, crackers, chips or pita wedges.

Bottled onion juice can be found in the baking/spice aisle of the grocery store. You can also make your own onion juice by "squeezing" an onion over a lemon juicer.

SOUTHERN ROSE RANCH

"Welcome to the Ranch!
Where a good rain and a new calf are always welcome."

A visitor to Southern Rose Ranch will get a glimpse of a simpler life and a slower pace. This is very much a working country ranch. The ranch breeds Belted Galloway cattle, also known as Oreo Cows or Texas Zebras. Their appearance is quite unusual.

Your stay at the ranch will include a gourmet breakfast made with farm-fresh eggs and herbs served in your private suite or in the outdoor kitchen.

This storybook ranch is perfect for the romantic couple's weekend or a "girlfriend getaway."

"In the midst of our hectic schedules, crowded highways and continuous lists of things to do, the memories of our time at Southern Rose Ranch will certainly bring a moment of R&R." —GUESTS

INNKEEPERS:	Donna and Steve Cummins
ADDRESS:	8580 Dairy Farm Road, Chappell Hill, Texas 77426
TELEPHONE:	(979) 251-7871; (979) 251-4028 cell
E-MAIL:	stay@SouthernRoseRanch.com
WEBSITE:	www.SouthernRoseRanch.com
ROOMS:	2 Rooms; Private baths
CHILDREN:	Unable to accommodate
PETS:	Not allowed; Resident pets

Goat Cheese with Pesto

Makes 10 to 12 Servings

*"This is a favorite appetizer for our guests—
and all our friends request it for our get-togethers."*
—INNKEEPER, *Southern Rose Ranch*

2–4 ounces soft goat cheese
¼ cup pesto sauce (jar variety)
2 tablespoons sundried tomatoes
   (jar variety, julienne)
¼ cup fresh basil, shredded
¼ cup pine nuts
Crackers or Ciabatta bread

Heat the broiler. Grease a 9-inch glass ovenproof pie plate. Spread goat cheese evenly over the bottom of the baking dish. Layer pesto over the cheese; sprinkle tomatoes over the top of the pest. Broil until bubbly, but do not burn. Remove from broiler; sprinkle basil and pine nuts over the top. Serve with your choice of crackers or bread cut into bite sizes.

THE INN AT CRAIG PLACE

Breakfast at the Inn at Craig Place is a treat to delight all of the senses. A three-course gourmet breakfast is served on the wrap-around porch, in the historic candle-lit dining room or in your own room. A sample menu might include fruit bruschetta and an asparagus omelet with hollandaise sauce, followed by a piece of decadent raspberry cream cheese coffee cake.

In the evening, you will arrive home to find your bed turned down, a bedtime treat, a rose and a chocolate on your pillow to hasten sweet dreams.

The Happily Ever After Suite is light and airy with an outdoor garden motif. The softly draped canopy bed satisfies the most romantic of hearts and a sunroom welcomes the new day.

INNKEEPERS: Gregg and Kelly Alba

ADDRESS: 117 West Craig Place, San Antonio, Texas 78212

TELEPHONE: (210) 736-1017; (877) 427-2447; (210) 737-1562

E-MAIL: stay@craigplace.com

WEBSITE: www.craigplace.com

ROOMS: 3 Rooms; 1 Suite; Private baths

CHILDREN: Age 12 and older welcome

PETS: Not allowed; Resident cat

Stuffed Edam

Makes 1 Cheese Ball

*This appetizer is best if the cheese mixture is made
a day in advance for full flavor development.
Serve with bagel chips or your favorite multi-grain cracker.*

1 whole Edam cheese (about 7 ounces)
¼ cup mayonnaise
2 teaspoons chopped green onion
2 tablespoons white wine
2 teaspoons chopped parsley
1 (8-ounce) package cream cheese
1½ tablespoons lemon juice

Cut a 1½-inch circle from the top of the cheese. Scoop out the center of the cheese, leaving about a 1/4-inch shell and the red wax coating intact. Cover and store in refrigerator until ready to use.

Put removed cheese in a food processor. Add mayonnaise, green onion, wine, parsley, cream cheese and lemon juice; process until smooth. Put cheese mixture into a bowl, cover and refrigerate overnight to allow the cheese to mellow.

The next day, spoon the cheese mixture back into the shell and serve.

WRIGLEY HOUSE
BED AND BREAKFAST

There has been a dwelling on the Wrigley House location since 1883 when the lot was incorporated in the Old Town Survey, but according to Sanborn historical maps, the present dwelling appeared sometime between 1912 and 1920. The house is a beautiful example of the era.

Located only two blocks from historic downtown Brenham with its antique stores, shops, and restaurants, it is the perfect base for exploring the Bluebonnet or Independence trails, and for access to Round Top Antique Fairs and the many local festivals. The Blue Bell Creamery, and the Monastery of St. Claire's Miniature Horses are popular tourist destinations.

The host uses local produce and products whenever possible—so look for Chappell Hill sausages, fresh vegetables, and eggs from free-range chickens (kept by neighbors) on your breakfast platter.

Corporate travelers will enjoy wireless Internet connection and free local and national phone calls.

INNKEEPER:	Marilynn Wrigley
ADDRESS:	506 South Park, Brenham, Texas 77833
TELEPHONE:	(979) 836-4346 phone and fax
E-MAIL:	info@wrigleyhouse.com
WEBSITE:	www.wrigleyhouse.com
ROOMS:	2 Rooms; 1 Cottage; Private baths
CHILDREN:	Age 12 and older welcome
PETS:	Not permitted

Pineapple and Nut Cheese Spread

Makes 1½ Cups

16 ounces cream cheese, softened
   you may substitute Neufchatel cheese)
1 (8½-ounce) can pineapple, drained
⅓ cup pecans or almonds, chopped
¼ cup green bell pepper, diced
2 tablespoons green onion, diced

In a large bowl, combine all ingredients: mix well. Cover and chill 3–4 hours or overnight. Set out at room temperature before serving. Mixture can also be formed into a ball and rolled in an additional cup of nuts. Good on whole-wheat toast, muffins, or bagels.

THE QUEEN ANNE

Built in 1905, the Queen Anne features original stained-glass windows, 12-foot ceilings, exquisite inlaid wood floors and pocket doors, and has many fine antiques throughout. The inn is ideally located within walking distance of the historic downtown, Galveston Strand shopping area, theaters, many fine and casual restaurants, cruise terminal and beaches.

The Queen Anne Bed and Breakfast provides an elegant setting for small, intimate parlor weddings and receptions for two to thirty people. The Queen Anne is ideally located by Galveston's cruise ship terminal for that much anticipated honeymoon cruise vacation!

"Your hospitality is exceeded only by the great food and the fabulous surroundings." —GUEST

INNKEEPERS:	Beth and George Ibarra
ADDRESS:	1915 Sealy Avenue, Galveston, Texas 77550
TELEPHONE:	(409) 763-7088; (888) 763-7088
E-MAIL:	stay@galvestonqueenanne.com
WEBSITE:	www.galvestonqueenanne.com
ROOMS:	5 Rooms; 1 Suite; Private baths
CHILDREN:	Age 12 and older welcome
PETS:	Not allowed

Jezebel Sauce

Makes 3 Cups

This zippy sauce is delicious served over cream cheese as an appetizer with crackers. The sauce also makes a wonderful glaze for ham.

1 (18-ounce) jar pineapple preserves
1 (18-ounce) jar apple jelly
1 (5-ounce) jar prepared yellow mustard
1 (5-ounce) jar prepared horseradish
1 (8-ounce) package cream cheese
 (block-style, not a tub)
Crackers, for serving

In a medium bowl, combine preserves, jelly, mustard and horse-radish; mix until smooth. Refrigerate until ready to use.

Put the block of cream cheese on a serving plate. Spoon some of the sauce over the cream cheese. Serve with crackers.

STONEY RIDGE RANCH

A romantic, upscale getaway with sweeping views of the Texas Hill Country makes this ranch a must see. It offers the perfect blend of activity and rest. There are walking and hiking areas, bird and wildlife watching, and ranching activities to enjoy. Spa treatments are soothing options after a busy day.

Picnics are available to take along on your hiking or horseback riding adventures.

Try one of the special Romance, Honeymoon or Rejuvenating Weekend packages.

INNKEEPERS:	Rollie and Steve Devlin
ADDRESS:	326 PR 2323, Hondo, Texas 78861
MAILING:	(PO Box 357) 78761
TELEPHONE:	(830) 562-3542; (210) 827-6776 cell; (830) 426-3939 fax
E-MAIL:	stonyridge@indian-creek.net
WEBSITE:	www.stonyridgeranch.com
ROOMS:	1 log home; 2 cabins; Private baths
CHILDREN:	Unable to accommodate
PETS:	Not allowed; Resident cats

Fresh Tomato and Avocado Towers

Makes 6 to 8 Servings

*This recipe calls for a little extra work ahead of time.
Preparing this special oil will take three days—keep this in mind
when you are planning this appetizer.*

OIL:
1 bottle of fresh extra virgin olive oil (12-ounces)
1 3–4-inch fresh rosemary sprig

Do Ahead: Pour out ¼ of the olive oil from the bottle; save in another jar. Add the rosemary sprig to the bottled oil; pour enough of the saved oil back into the bottle to completely cover the rosemary. Let the rosemary oil sit for at least 3 days to develop its flavor.

TOMATOES AND AVOCADOS:
3 yellow medium tomatoes
3 red ripe medium tomatoes
2 large Hass avocados
3 small key limes, juiced
Sea salt and cracked fresh pepper, to taste
Blue corn tortillas, for dipping

In preparation: Carefully cut the tomatoes into ¼-inch slices and set aside. Cut the avocados in half and remove the seed and skin. Cut into ¼-inch slices so that there is a nice slice with a hole in the middle; set aside. Sprinkle the key-lime juice over the avocado slices; sprinkle with just a little salt and pepper.

To assemble: On an hors d'oeuvre plate alternately layer an avocado slice, a red tomato slice, and a yellow tomato slice. You should have 12 to 15 individual stacks. Drizzle with rosemary olive oil and garnish with a sprig of rosemary stuck in the top of the tomato. Sprinkle with additional sea salt and cracked pepper. Serve a blue corn chip on the side of the plate.

THE TEXAS WHITE HOUSE

Whether its the culture of the Kimball, performances at the Bass, the Cowgirl Hall of Fame or the nightlife—Fort Worth has something for everyone. Guests find more than enough to keep them busy for days.

The innkeepers will help honeymooners and guests celebrating anniversaries design their own romance packages, including the finest special-occasion suites, breakfast served in the room and horse-drawn carriage rides.

Business guests will appreciate the close proximity to downtown Fort Worth and the Medical District. Everyone will benefit from the stress relieving, therapeutic, on-site massage services.

The names of the rooms and suites are as Texas as you can get: the Longhorn Suite, Mustang Suite, Tejas Room, Lone Star Room, and the Land of Contrast Room.

INNKEEPERS: Jamie and Grover McMains
ADDRESS: 1417 Eighth Avenue, Fort Worth, Texas 76104
TELEPHONE: (817) 923-3597; (800) 279-6491; (817) 923-0410 fax
E-MAIL: stay@texaswhitehouse.com
WEBSITE: www.texaswhitehouse.com
ROOMS: 3 Rooms; 2 Suites; Private baths
CHILDREN: Welcome
PETS: Call ahead

Pecan-Crusted Sausage Balls

Makes 20 to 24 Appetizers

"A great make-ahead recipe. These appetizers freeze well."
—INNKEEPER, *The Texas White House*

> 1 pound bulk sausage
> 2 (8-ounce) cups pecan pieces

Preheat oven to 350°F. Toast pecan pieces in the oven for 8–10 minutes, stirring and checking frequently. Be careful that they do not burn.

Roll sausage into bite-size balls and coat with toasted pecans. Bake for 25 minutes, or until sausage is completely cooked.

SUNSET INN

Visitors to the Sunset Inn will be pampered with food, quiet time, and magnificent scenery. Meals are considered an event—serving breakfast, lunch if requested, and dinner on Saturdays. Meal times are designed to be a throwback to the "good old times" when friends dined and conversed on life in general, the arts, the day's events, and the future of the universe.

"Retreat time" offers the chance to sit on the porches and relax, enjoy hors d'oeuvres and drinks, and watch the sun retreat. The inn sits on a site that has commanding views of the "Divide"—the Texas Hill Country at its best.

INNKEEPER:	Jane Gay
ADDRESS:	124 Oehler Road, Ingram, Texas 78025
TELEPHONE:	(830) 866-3336; (877) 739-1214; (830) 866-3445
E-MAIL:	janegay@ktc.com
WEBSITE:	www.sunsetinn-studio.com
ROOMS:	2 Rooms; Private baths
CHILDREN:	Age 16 and older welcome
PETS:	Not allowed; Resident dog, Longhorns, donkeys and deer

Sausage Crostini

Makes 8 to 10 Servings

1 pound pan sausage (2 cups cooked)
2 loaves French bread
4 tablespoons butter, melted
1 white onion (½ cup), finely diced
1 red bell pepper (½ cup), finely diced
1 (8-ounce) package cream cheese, softened
1½ cups cheese, grated (choose from cheddar,
    Monterey Jack, Queso Quesadlla, Asadero)

Spray the bottom and sides of a 12-inch skillet with cooking spray. Cook sausage; drain and set aside. Slice bread into ½- to ¾-inch slices. Brush tops of bread with butter. Place bread on baking sheet(s) and broil until tops are golden brown. Remove and set oven to 350°F.

In a food processor, combine ½ cup onion, ½ cup red pepper, sausage, cream cheese, and grated cheese; process until blended. Place 1 large tablespoon of sausage mixture on each slice of toast; spread evenly. Bake 5 minutes to warm. This can also be spread on crackers.

Chicken Quesadillas

Makes 30 to 40 Wedges

3 chicken breasts, skinless, boneless
1 (14.5-ounce) can chicken broth
1 (10-ounce) can Rotel Tomatoes & Green Chilies
1 bunch green onions, diced for ½ cup
1 (16-ounce) box Velveeta cheese
1 10-count package 10-inch tortillas
1 (16-ounce) can Old El Paso Refried Beans Fat Free
Ground black pepper, to taste (suggest Adams Malabar)
Salsa, guacamole, sour cream, to serve
Slice chicken breasts lengthwise, about ¼-inch in width.
   Cut strips in small pieces and set aside.

Drain tomatoes; reserve liquid; set both aside. Cut cheese into chunks and place in a covered dish; add tomatoes. Microwave for 2½ minutes; remove and stir. Microwave another 2½ minutes; remove and stir; add chicken and onions to cheese mixture; mix well.

Spray bottom of a 10-or12-inch skillet with cooking spray; heat medium to high. Spread 1 tablespoon refried beans on ½ of one side of each tortilla. Place tortilla in the skillet with refried beans facing up. Pour ⅔ cup of chicken/cheese mixture over refried beans and fold the other side over to cover. Mash the edges of the tortilla together with edge of spatula to help seal the tortilla. Cook until tortilla is brown, approximately 1 minute, turn and cook other side until brown. Remove from skillet, place on plate and allow to cool. Repeat for each tortillas. Cut each tortilla in half, then cut each half into two "Vs" or wedges.

Tip:
Allow the quesadillas to chill in the refrigerator for a few minutes before cutting into wedges. It will prevent the cheese from running out. After cutting, place on a baking sheet sprayed with cooking spray and warm briefly in 300°F oven before serving.

Crunchy Chicken Tenders

Makes 4 to 6 Servings

1 chicken breast, skinless, boneless
2 cups bran flakes or cornflakes
1 teaspoon Italian seasoning
½ teaspoon salt
½ teaspoon ground black pepper
    (suggest Adams Malabar)
1 egg
4 tablespoons butter

Preheat oven to 400°F. Spray the bottom and sides of a 9x13-inch baking dish with cooking spray. Cover the sides and bottom with aluminum foil. Coat foil with cooking spray.

Cut chicken into pieces approximately 1-inch long and ⅓-inch wide. Set aside.

Place bran flakes in a 1-quart plastic sealable bag. Crush flakes. Add Italian seasoning, salt and pepper; shake well to mix. Place flakes mixture in a bowl. In a shallow bowl, whisk egg. Dip chicken parts in egg and coat with flake mixture; place chicken in baking dish when coated. Drizzle melted butter over chicken. Bake for 20 minutes or until an internal temperature of 165°F is reached. Serve with a honey-mustard dressing, cocktail sauce, or marinara sauce.

HONEY MUSTARD DRESSING:
¾ cup mayonnaise
2 tablespoons Grey Poupon Dijon Mustard
¼ cup honey

In a small bowl, combine all ingredients; whisk well to mix. Keep chilled until ready to use.

Wisteria Hideaway

Wisteria Hideaway Bed and Breakfast, in the heart of the Piney Woods of Deep East Texas, is a 1939 Colonial-style home that provides an oasis of Southern hospitality and warmth. The majestic splendor of the four-acre Lufkin estate will impress travelers looking for privacy and convenience.

Let the wisteria-laden forests, pine floors and large-columned front porch welcome you comfortably into this grand inn. Whether you choose the Calloway Room with its rich red walls, the bright and sunny Ivy Room, the light and airy Garden Room, or the Master Suite, you will be treated to comfort and luxury—and most of all—privacy.

INNKEEPERS:	Ron and Brenda A.Cole
ADDRESS:	3458 Ted Trout Drive, Lufkin, Texas 75904
TELEPHONE:	(936) 875-2914; (936) 875-2915
E-MAIL:	info@wisteriahideaway.com
WEBSITE:	www.wisteriahideaway.com
ROOMS:	3 Rooms; 1 Suite; Private baths
CHILDREN:	Welcome
PETS:	Not allowed; Resident outdoor cat

Clear Punch

Makes 5 Cups Punch Concentrate
(enough to make 2½ gallons of punch)

*Each 1 cup of punch concentrate makes 2 quarts of punch
when mixed with ginger ale. For added color,
float an ice ring of mixed fruits or berries in the punch.
This punch is perfect for showers, wedding receptions
or any type of special celebration. If clear vanilla extract
is not available at your grocery store, you may find it at
cake decorating stores, gourmet groceries, Sam's Club or Costco.*

5 cups sugar
2 cups water
1 (1-ounce) bottle almond extract
1 (1-ounce) bottle clear vanilla extract
½ cup lemon juice
Ginger ale (2-10 quarts, depending
on the amount of punch being made)

In a saucepan, heat sugar and water over medium heat. Cook and
stir until sugar is dissolved. Remove from heat; stir in the almond
extract, vanilla extract and lemon juice. Cool. (At this point, the
concentrate can be divided into 1 cup portions and refrigerated
for use within a few days, or frozen for longer storage.)

To make punch, mix 1 cup concentrate with 2 quarts of ginger
ale. Pour into a punch bowl and add an ice ring. To serve, ladle
into punch cups.

ANT STREET INN

In historic Brenham, home to Bluebonnets and Blue Bell Ice Cream, a great old building is seeing its rebirth as a premier historic inn. The Ant Street Inn combines the finest in Deep South hospitality, warmth and elegance with the conveniences and the personal service of a first-class hotel.

Relax in rocking chairs on the back balcony overlooking the courtyard, enjoy the many shops, restaurants and night spots in the historic Ant Street area or dine at the Ant Street Inn's Capital Grill.

INNKEEPERS: Pam and Tommy Traylor
ADDRESS: 107 West Commerce Street, Brenham, Texas 77833
TELEPHONE: (979) 836-7393; (800) 481-1951
E-MAIL: stay@antstreetinn.com
WEBSITE: www.antstreetinn.com
ROOMS: 14 Rooms; Private baths
CHILDREN: Age 12 and older welcome
PETS: Not allowed

Hot Mulled Cider

Makes 8 Servings

"Social time in the winter months at the Ant Street Inn always features this hot apple drink. My husband, Tommy, had a habit of drinking multiple cups of cider, and usually drank most of it before the guests could get any! One time, I thought I could hide the cider from Tommy by heating a percolator of cider inside a storage area. The coffee pot started 'moaning' as some older pots will do. Tommy heard the moaning and thought a guest was having a problem. I had to confess that I was just hiding the cider from him, and he could have one cup."
—PAM TRAYLOR, *Innkeeper, Ant Street Inn*

½ cup brown sugar, packed
1 teaspoon whole allspice
1 teaspoon whole cloves
1/4 teaspoon salt
Dash of ground nutmeg
1 cinnamon stick (about 3-inches long)
2 quarts apple cider
Orange wedges, for garnish
Additional whole cloves, for garnish

Put brown sugar, allspice, cloves, salt, nutmeg and cinnamon stick in a piece of cheesecloth or a coffee filter. Tie with a piece of kitchen twine to secure. Pour apple cider in a large saucepan and add the spice "bag". Bring the cider to a boil over medium heat. Lower heat, cover and simmer gently for 20 minutes. Remove the spice bag and discard. Serve the cider in warmed mugs with a clove-studded orange wedge in each cup for garnish.

NOTE:
You can also make this recipe in a clean, large coffee percolator. Put the spices in the coffee filter and fill the percolator with the cider. The percolator keeps the cider warm while serving.

Lunch & Dinner Entrées

Lunch & Dinner Entrées

> "One cannot think well,
> love well, sleep well,
> if one has not dined well."
>
> —VIRGINIA WOOLF

ROCKIN RIVER INN

The Rockin River Inn is located on the Guadalupe River, central to the Texas Hill Country. The inn is surrounded by Hill Country native landscapes that display a Texas wildflower show in spring, and a spectacular changing of the leaves in fall.

Rockin River guests can enjoy tubing, kayaking, canoeing, biking, antiquing, motorcycling, museums, wineries, bird watching, hunting, fishing, stargazing, Lost Maples Wilderness Area, Sea World, the Alamo, and more!

INNKEEPER:	Ken Wardlaw
ADDRESS:	103 Skyline Road, Center Point, Texas 78010
TELEPHONE:	(830) 634-7043; (866) 424-0576
E-MAIL:	relax@rockinriverinn.com
WEBSITE:	www.rockinriverinn.com
ROOMS:	3 Rooms; 1 Suite; Private baths
CHILDREN:	Welcome
PETS:	Not allowed; Resident dog

River-Sitting Sunshine Soup

Makes 8 to 10 Appetizer Servings

"When the river gets low in July and August,
we invite guests to sit in the river for afternoon cocktails.
A favorite river-sitting cocktail treat is this
refreshing cold soup that's as healthy as the sunshine
that sparkles off the Guadalupe River."
—INNKEEPER, *Rockin River Inn*

1 (64-ounce) bottle Clamato juice

6–8 ounces firm tofu, drained
    and cut into $1/3$-inch cubes

$1/3$ cup (more or less) onion or green onion,
    finely chopped

2 small-to-medium avocados,
    cut into $1/3$-inch cubes

½ cup chopped celery

1 large cucumber, peeled, seeded
    and cut into $1/3$-inch cubes

6–8 ounces frozen salad shrimp
    (thaw quickly by rinsing with cold water,
    drain and pat dry with paper towel)

4 tablespoons red wine vinegar

2 tablespoons extra-virgin olive oil

1–2 teaspoons sugar, to taste

Salt and pepper, to taste

In a very large pot or container, combine all ingredients; stir well. Cover and refrigerate overnight, or for at least 8 hours.

Serve in wine glasses or clear plastic cups to enjoy the deep red color. Provide spoons for getting out every last bite.

BED ROX

The pet-friendly, child-friendly, and smoke-free Bed Rox is in central Texas, fifteen miles outside of Austin. The inn is comprised of three individual dwellings: The Main House, The Little Rox, and Villa Le Franc.

Set among native live oaks on scenic Lake Travis, The Little Rox is a small abode that must have originated from a vision of the perfect hideaway and then built with a good dose of whimsical joy. Luminarias are the subtle light source leading to the terra cotta colored cabin. Inside The Little Rox, there are cast iron spur curtain rod hangers, pewter Texas stars suspending the shower curtain, and a breeze created by the hand-carved wooden blades of a ceiling fan.

Budget Living magazine says: "Try the best little house in Texas: The Little Rox, a wonderfully quirky cabin that sleeps four."

The spacious main house sits on five-and-a-half secluded acres, boasts a Texas-style hot tub, gas barbeque grill, picnic table, horseshoe pit and a chiminea for romantic, chilly nights.

Villa Le Franc features a wonderfully unconventional water feature.

INNKEEPER: Roxann Johnson
ADDRESS: 5113 Doss Road, Austin, Texas 78734
TELEPHONE: (512) 266-3560; (866) 249-8325
E-MAIL: Rox@thebedrox.com
WEBSITE: www.thebedrox.com
ROOMS: 3 Cottages; Private baths
CHILDREN: Welcome
PETS: Welcome; Resident dog and two miniature donkeys

Bed Rox Homemade Chicken Noodle Soup

Makes 4 to 6 Servings

SOUP:

1 whole chicken

2 gallons of water

4 celery stalks

1 large white onion

3 cloves of garlic

24 ounces chicken broth

2 tablespoons Chef Paul Prudhomme's
    Vegetable Magic

1 (8-ounce) container sour cream

Egg Noodles: The amount of cooked noodles you will need for this soup is variable, depending on your taste. We suggest a cup per serving. You may use your favorite recipe for homemade noodles, or use packaged egg noodles.

In a large soup pot, combine all ingredients with the exception of the sour cream and noodles. Boil the chicken until the meat falls off the bone. Take the chicken out of the pot; let cool and remove all remaining meat from the bone. Once the chicken is out of the pot, add the noodles and cook for an additional 15 minutes. Add the remaining chicken; turn off the heat; cool down slightly. Add the sour cream and stir. Serve warm.

> *Soup is liquid comfort.*
>
> —ANONYMOUS

THE ANGLIN ROSE

Nestled among centuries-old oak trees in the town of Cleburne, The Anglin Rose has recently been restored to its original 1892 elegance. This painted lady Victorian features three fireplaces, an octagonal second-floor turret, and an original stained-glass key-hole window. Within an hours drive of Dallas and thirty minutes from Ft. Worth, this residence was built for John Luther and Annie

Cleveland, owners of Cleburne Cotton-seed Oil Mill and the Cleveland Hardware store. Mr. Cleveland was instrumental in bringing the railroad to Cleburne.

Select Uncle Sam's room or Grandma's room for your overnight stay. An attic playroom filled with Victorian-era toys awaits you in Uncle Sam's room. Grandma's room is extra large and includes a sitting room and a king-size bed covered with a handmade yoyo quilt.

The magical atmosphere and intimate setting at the Anglin Rose are available for wedding parties. There are three romantic packages from which to choose.

INNKEEPER:	Saundra Williams
ADDRESS:	808 South Anglin Street, Cleburne, Texas 76031
TELEPHONE:	(817) 641-7433
E-MAIL:	anglinrose@htcomp.net
WEBSITE:	www.users.htcomp.net/anglinrose
ROOMS:	2 Rooms; Private baths; one located across the hall
CHILDREN:	Unable to accommodate
PETS:	Not allowed

Chicken Salad Anglin Rose Style

Makes 15 Servings

"Gets rave reviews!"
—INNKEEPER, *Anglin Rose*

3 pounds boneless chicken breasts
1 teaspoon salt
½ teaspoon pepper
1 teaspoon seasoning salt
1 onion, chopped
1 (8-ounce) package cream cheese, softened
1 cup mayonnaise
1 cup walnuts or almonds, chopped
1 tablespoon tarragon
1 (6-ounce) package dried cranberries
Celery, chopped very fine (optional)

In a large pot, cover chicken with water and cook with salt
and pepper, seasoning salt, and onion until tender and cooked
through. Drain; reserving ½ cup of broth. Cool chicken and cut
into 1-inch pieces; set aside.

In a large bowl, combine cream cheese, mayonnaise, nuts,
cranberries, tarragon and celery; stirring until well blended.
Add chicken. Stir in small amounts of broth if the dressing
is too thick. Serve chilled.

STONEY RIDGE RANCH

Aromantic, upscale getaway with sweeping views of the Texas Hill Country makes this ranch a must see. It offers the perfect blend of activity and rest. There are walking and hiking areas, bird and wildlife watching, and ranching activities to enjoy. Spa treatments are soothing options after a busy day.

Picnics are available to take along on your hiking or horseback riding adventures.

Try one of the special Romance, Honeymoon or Rejuvenating Weekend packages.

INNKEEPERS:	Rollie and Steve Devlin
ADDRESS:	326 PR 2323, Hondo, Texas 78861
MAILING:	PO Box 357
TELEPHONE:	(830) 562-3542; (830) 426-3939 fax
E-MAIL:	stonyridge@indian-creek.net
WEBSITE:	www.stonyridgeranch.com
ROOMS:	3 Cottages; Private baths
CHILDREN:	Unable to accommodate
PETS:	Not allowed; Resident cats

Grilled Chicken on Rosemary Branches with Lavender Honey

Makes 6 to 8 Servings

The lavender honey needs to be made at least 24 hours ahead of time. It stores well up for up to 6 months—and makes a great gift. The chicken shish ke-bob recipe is quite unusual—and takes some effort to find the rosemary branches—but it will wow your guests.

DO AHEAD: LAVENDER HONEY:

2 cups raw honey
1 tablespoon dried lavender buds
or 25 flowering lavender sprigs, 3-inch long

In a small saucepan, add the honey and stir on low heat until very warm. Stir in the lavender; remove from heat and cover. It should sit in the pan for at least 24 hours.

When you are ready to serve it, warm on low heat, until it is thin enough to pour. Whatever you are not going to use right away, pour into a clean jar with a tight-fitting lid and store for up to 6 months.

GRILLED CHICKEN:

1 pound chicken tenders
¼ cup olive oil
1 tablespoon dark brown sugar
2 cloves garlic
Salt and pepper, to taste
25–30 fresh rosemary branches, 6-8 inches long
Lavender sprigs and flowers for garnish

Wash chicken well; pat dry with paper towels. Place chicken in a large resealable freezer bag; add olive oil, brown sugar, garlic, salt and pepper. Marinate for 2-3 hours in the refrigerator. On a foil-lined baking sheet, lay out the chicken; skewer the chicken tenders with the rosemary branches. Grill on low heat for 2 minutes per side, or until done. Watch them carefully so they do not burn. Remove from heat; brush well with lavender honey; garnish plates with lavender sprigs or extra flowers; serve.

ANT STREET INN

The 14 guest rooms at the Ant Street Inn have been painstakingly restored by artisans to retain their original flavor while offering the best in modern comfort and convenience. Rooms feature 12-foot ceilings, polished hardwood floors, and Oriental rugs.

The innkeepers have scoured the country to create a superb collection of American antiques, including the inn's exquisite and romantic beds. Some rooms offer sitting areas, desks, stained-glass windows and two-person tubs, reminiscent of the grand lifestyle of the 1890s.

INNKEEPERS: Pam and Tommy Traylor
ADDRESS: 107 West Commerce Street, Brenham, Texas 77833
TELEPHONE: (979) 836-7393; (800) 481-1951
E-MAIL: stay@antstreetinn.com
WEBSITE: www.antstreetinn.com
ROOMS: 14 Rooms; Private baths
CHILDREN: Age 12 and older welcome
PETS: Not allowed

Puffed Chicken Alouette

Makes 6 Servings

*"This recipe is a quick favorite for family and friends.
It has a very elegant presentation and looks much more
difficult to prepare than it is."*
—INNKEEPER, *Ant Street Inn*

1 (17-ounce) package frozen puff pastry sheets, thawed
1 (6 ½-ounce) container Alouette Garlic
    and Herb Spreadable Cheese
6 boneless, skinless chicken breast halves
Salt and pepper, to taste
Egg wash (1 egg beaten with 1 tablespoon water)

Preheat oven to 400°F. Unfold pastry sheets. On a floured surface, roll each sheet into a 12x14-inch rectangle. Cut the first pastry sheet into four 6x7-inch rectangles. Cut the second sheet in half. Cut two 6x7-inch rectangles from ½ of the sheet. Cut 24 thin (about ¼-inch wide) strips from the other ½ of the sheet.

Spread ¹/₆ of the spreadable cheese onto each chicken breast. Sprinkle with salt and pepper. Place 1 chicken breast, cheese-side-down, onto the center of each 6x7-inch pastry rectangle. Brush water onto the edges of the pastry, which extend beyond the chicken. Pull the edges of the pastry up around the chicken, overlapping the edges to secure. Place bundles, seam-side-down onto a lightly greased baking sheet.

Twist 2 of the ¼-inch strips of dough gently together into a braid. Place lengthwise on a chicken breast bundle, tucking the ends under the bundle. Twist 2 more strips together and place them crosswise across the bundle. Repeat with the remaining strips of dough for each chicken bundle. (If you are not baking the chicken right away, you can cover and refrigerate the bundles for up to 2 hours.)

Preheat oven to 400°F. Brush egg wash over the top and sides of each bundle (this helps the pastries become a beautiful, golden brown). Bake for 25 minutes, or until bundles are golden brown.

THE INN OF MANY FACES

Located 70 miles north of Dallas, on the Oklahoma border near Lake Texoma, the Inn of Many Faces is not only a great place to relax, but the location also offers easy access to fishing and boating on the lake, several area golf courses, antique and art browsing in downtown Denison and much more.

For the less ambitious, spend your afternoons relaxing on the great porch, catching fireflies in the garden, or feeding the goldfish in the garden pond.

INNKEEPERS:	Charlie and Gloria Morton
ADDRESS:	412 West Morton Street, Denison, Texas 75020
TELEPHONE:	(903) 465-4639
E-MAIL:	BandB@innofmanyfaces.com
WEBSITE:	www.innofmanyfaces.com
ROOMS:	4 Rooms; Private baths
CHILDREN:	Age 11 and older welcome
PETS:	Not allowed

Poppy Seed Chicken in Puff Pastry

Makes 12 Servings

*"We serve this dish at luncheons and showers—
it always receives rave reviews."*
—INNKEEPER, *The Inn of Many Faces*

2 (10-ounce) packages Pepperidge Farm frozen
    puff pastry shells (12 puff pastry shells total)
4–5 boneless, skinless chicken breast halves,
    cooked and chopped
1 (26-ounce) can condensed cream of chicken soup
1 (26-ounce) can condensed cream of mushroom soup
24 ounces sour cream
4 tablespoons poppy seeds
1 cup slivered almonds
Fresh parsley, for garnish (optional)

Bake the 12 puff pastry shells according to package directions; set aside.

Reduce oven heat to 350°F. Spray a 9x13-inch baking dish with nonstick cooking spray. In a large bowl, combine cooked, chopped chicken and both soups; pour into baking dish. Bake, uncovered, for 50–60 minutes. Add sour cream, poppy seeds, and slivered almonds; stir to mix thoroughly. Bake for 15–20 minutes more.

Place the bottom half of each pastry shell on each plate. Fill with the hot chicken mixture, overflowing the mixture onto the plate. Top with the pastry puff lid. Garnish with parsley, if desired.

GREEN GABLES

Located just 30 miles north of San Antonio and 60 miles west of Austin, Green Gables is central to many Texas Hill Country sites and events, and is the perfect jumping-off point for exploring nearby Fredericksburg, Johnson City, and Boerne.

In Anne's Rose Cottage, enjoy a soothing soak in the antique claw-foot tub with special bath amenities by Crabtree & Evelyn, or snuggle up on the loveseat with your special someone in front of the gas log fireplace.

"A beautiful cozy cottage in a quiet country landscape...
Thank you for your warm hospitality and the comfortable
personal touches at the cottage." —GUEST

INNKEEPERS:	Glen and Sue McFarlin
ADDRESS:	401 Green Gables, Blanco, Texas 78606
TELEPHONE:	(830) 833-5931; (888) 833-5931; (830) 833-5944 fax
E-MAIL:	info@greengables-tx.com
WEBSITE:	www.greengables-tx.com
ROOMS:	1 Suite; 2 Cottages; Private baths
CHILDREN:	Welcome
PETS:	Not allowed; Resident dogs & cats

African Curry

Makes 6 Servings

*This wonderful curry dish is a great way
to use leftover turkey or chicken. If you prefer,
boil fresh poultry until cooked through. Serve over rice.*

2 tablespoons butter or oil
1 onion, chopped
2–3 fresh tomatoes, chopped
2 tablespoons curry powder
$\frac{1}{8}$ teaspoon cayenne pepper
$\frac{1}{2}$ teaspoon salt
4 tablespoons flour
2 cups chicken broth
2 cups de-boned, chopped cooked chicken or turkey
Condiments: Shredded coconut, crushed pineapple,
    chopped hard-boiled eggs, chutney, chopped
    salted peanuts, raisins and chopped tomatoes
Cooked rice, for serving

In a large pan, gently heat butter or oil. Add onion, tomato, curry powder, cayenne and salt; cook until onions are soft. Add flour, stir to coat and cook for 2 more minutes. Add chicken broth and bring to a simmer. Cook until sauce is a medium-thick consistency. Add turkey or chicken; simmer to heat through (if sauce is too thick, add a little more chicken broth or water).

Spoon condiments into small, individual bowls and place on dining table. Put rice into soup or pasta bowls and ladle the curry over the rice. Let guests add their own condiments.

Blair House

 **B**lair House is a fine country inn that offers something for everyone. Whether you are looking for rest and relaxation, a stimulating writer's retreat or a cooking class, look no further! The food at this inn is magnificent. Chef Christopher Stonesifer recently won second prize in the annual Taste of San Antonio culinary competition.

The Cooking School at Blair House offers classes year round. It is a hands-on environment, so wear comfortable clothes and come ready to get your hands in the dough.

Each guest room and cottage at Blair House Inn is individually and uniquely designed. Every room has fresh flowers, fine chocolates, and cozy robes. Most rooms have wireless Internet access or guests may use the workstation in the library.

"A five-star dining experience…
the place to stay in Wimberley."
—D Magazine

INNKEEPERS: Mike and Vickie Schneider
ADDRESS: 100 West Spoke Hill Road, Wimberley, Texas 78676
TELEPHONE: (512) 847-1111; (877) 549-5450
E-MAIL: info@blairhouseinn.com
WEBSITE: www.blairhouseinn.com
ROOMS: 8 Rooms; 3 Cottages; Private baths
CHILDREN: Age 14 and older welcome
PETS: Not allowed; Resident dog

Guajillo-Rubbed, Herb-Smoked Muscovy Duck Breast

Makes 4 Servings

3 guajillo chilies (dark red dried chilies),
   or dried ancho or poblano chilies
½ cup olive oil
5 cloves garlic
1 tablespoon cumin
⅓ cup kosher salt
1 tablespoon cracked black peppercorns
4 (6-ounce) Muscovy duck breasts
   (or other thick, fatty-skinned duck breasts)
Large handful of each fresh herb: rosemary, thyme,
   marjoram, oregano, or other herbs of choice
   (soak herbs in water for 1 hour before using)

HONEY AND BLACKBERRY COULIS:
   [koo-LEE] (a thick, pureed sauce):
¼ cup tequila
1 cup honey
2 pints blackberries

Blend dried chilies, olive oil, garlic, cumin, salt and peppercorns in a blender until smooth. Cut or score diamonds into skin of duck breasts. Rub thoroughly on both sides with chile mixture. Chill breasts for at least 20 minutes, or overnight. Prep a smoker or BBQ grill for the indirect heat. Place soaked herbs on coals. Smoke duck breasts in smoker for 20 minutes.

Heat a heavy skillet over medium-high heat. Sear duck breasts skin-side-down in skillet for 10–15 minutes, until skin is golden and crisp, and fat is rendered. Turn and sear the meat side for 1 minute; remove from heat and let rest for 5 minutes. Slice duck breasts diagonally; keep warm.

While duck is searing, prepare coulis (or prepare coulis ahead and warm before serving). Bring tequila to a boil over medium-high heat; reduce to a glaze (this takes just a few minutes). Add honey and blackberries. Heat for 3–5 minutes, then whirl in a blender until smooth. Press mixture through a sieve; discard seeds. Keep mixture warm. To serve, spread plates with coulis. Put duck slices on top of sauce. Garnish with mint sprigs.

Chef Christopher's Brisket East-Texas Style

Makes 8 to 10 Servings

5 quarts (20 cups) good beef stock
2 cups dry red wine
2 bay leaves
1 tablespoon whole black peppercorns
3 cloves garlic, lightly crushed
¼ cup Kosher or sea salt
1 (4- to 5-pound) beef brisket, fat cap on
1¼ cups favorite barbecue sauce,
    plus additional for serving

In a large stockpot, combine beef stock, wine, bay leaves, peppercorns, garlic and salt. Bring the mixture to a low boil. Place the brisket in the boiling liquid and cook at a low simmer until tender, about 1½ hours.

Remove the meat from the liquid and place on the top rack of a grill or smoker. Smoke for 60 minutes, basting with barbecue sauce. Let brisket rest on a cutting board for 15 minutes. Trim excess fat and slice the brisket very thinly across the grain. Serve with additional barbecue sauce, if desired.

I know vegetarians don't like

to hear this, but God made

an awful lot of land that's good

for nothing but grazing.

—MOLLY IVINS

Chili-Marinated Flank Steak

Makes 6 Servings

½ cup red wine vinegar
⅓ cup olive oil
¼ cup chili powder
2½ tablespoons garlic powder
2½ tablespoons Hungarian sweet paprika
1 tablespoon salt
2 tablespoons packed brown sugar
½ cup red onion, chopped
1 large or 2 small bay leaves, crumbled
1 fresh thyme sprig
1 fresh rosemary sprig
1 (2-pound) flank steak
3 cups mesquite chips, soaked in water for 1 hour
Caramelized onions (recipe follows)

In a medium bowl, whisk together vinegar, olive oil, chili powder, garlic powder, paprika, salt, and brown sugar (the mixture will be thick). Add onion, bay leaves, thyme and rosemary. Put steak in a glass-baking dish. Spread ½ of marinade over top of meat. Turn and coat the other side with the remaining marinade. Cover with plastic wrap. Refrigerate for at least 1 day and up to 2 days.

When ready to cook, heat grill to medium-high heat. Drain mesquite chips and sprinkle over coals (or put in a smoker box). Brush grill rack with oil. Scrape almost all of the marinade off the meat; discard marinade. Grill steak to desired doneness, about 4 minutes per side for medium-rare. Transfer steak to a cutting board; let stand for 5 minutes. Slice steak diagonally, across the grain, into very thin slices. Serve with caramelized onions.

CARAMELIZED ONIONS:

2 tablespoons olive oil
2 tablespoons butter
2 onions, thinly sliced into rings
2 teaspoons sugar

Heat olive oil and butter in a skillet over medium to medium-high heat. Add onions; cook until starting to brown, about 5 minutes. Lower heat to medium-low, sprinkle with sugar and cook for 10–15 minutes more, until golden and tender. Season with salt and pepper.

THE COOK'S COTTAGE & SUITES

Innkeeper Patsy Bynum Swendson is a nationally recognized authority on Southwestern cuisine who has delighted radio and television audiences for over 20 years, authored 49 cookbooks and has been a contributing writer for nine national magazines.

If gourmet dining is high on your list while staying at a bed and breakfast, then this is the place for you. Some of Patsy's recipes

featured in other cookbooks include: Tortilla Turtles, Enchilada Suizas, Gringo Migas, and Texas Sunburst. What are these wonderful delights?

Located in the heart of the Texas Hill Country, The Cook's Cottage has been selected by *Travel and Leisure* magazine as "One of the Top 25 Most Romantic Places in the U.S."

The Cook's Cottage & Suites provides privacy, romance and attention to every detail. Located just one block from Fredericksburg's Main Street, this is the perfect setting to celebrate a special occasion.

"The Cook's Cottage's one-room guesthouse is one of those rare places where you feel like the outside world doesn't exist, let alone matter."

—COUNTRY HOME

INNKEEPER: Patsy Swendson

ADDRESS: 703 West Austin, Fredericksburg, Texas 78624

TELEPHONE: (210) 493-5101; (888) 991-6749; (866) 869-0364 fax

E-MAIL: patsyswendson@yahoo.com

WEBSITE: www.bed-inn-breakfast-tx.com

ROOMS: 3 Rooms; 2 Suites; 1 Cottage; Private baths

CHILDREN: Unable to accommodate

PETS: Not allowed

Pan-Fried Pork with Peaches

Makes 4 Servings

*"A delightful breakfast or brunch dish that will have your guests
in the palm of your hand. The addition of the peaches is a
great way to utilize those wonderful Fredericksburg peaches
so prevalent and fragrant in the summer months."*
—INNKEEPER, *The Cook's Cottage & Suites*

2 tablespoons flour
Salt and pepper, to taste
4 (¼-inch thick) pork loin cutlets
3 tablespoons vegetable oil
2 tablespoons sherry
2 green onions, minced
1 tablespoon green peppercorns
¼ cup chicken stock
    (use up to ½ cup if a thinner sauce is desired)
3 large ripe peaches, peeled and sliced
½ lemon, juiced
Fresh mint leaves, for garnish
Spiced apples, for garnish

On a plate, combine flour, salt and pepper; dredge pork cutlets on
both sides in the flour mixture. In a large skillet, heat oil; quickly fry
the pork on both sides, until just cooked through, about 4–6 minutes.
Transfer meat to a plate and cover with foil to keep warm.

Deglaze pan with sherry, stirring up any bits that cling to the
bottom of the pan. Stir in green onions and green peppercorns;
heat through. Add ¼ cup chicken stock and heat rapidly to reduce
and slightly thicken. Just before serving, return the meat to the
pan. Gently add the peach slices and heat through. Drizzle with
the juice from ½ lemon. Serve immediately, garnished with mint
leaves and spiced apples.

OCEAN HOUSE

The Ocean House is so much more than what you would expect in a bed and breakfast. It's an 8,000-square-foot magnificent contemporary Mediterranean-style home (the main house was built in 1936), with a wine cellar a Master Sommelier would approve of, plus a gorgeous tropical garden and pool area.

It offers a choice of five handsomely appointed suites. Each suite is a one bedroom with an adjoining living area and bath.

The Ocean House is conveniently located close to many area attractions. Whether it is golfing, tennis, fishing, birding, or browsing stores and art museums, the innkeeper will be happy to assist you in making arrangements or giving suggestions.

The Island Fun Package will have you ready for a day at the beach—a picnic basket is packed with food and drink, blankets, towels, and even sunscreen!

INNKEEPER: Stan Shoemaker
ADDRESS: 3275 Ocean Drive, Corpus Christi, Texas 78404
TELEPHONE: (361) 882-9500
E-MAIL: stan@oceanhousecorpuschristi.com
WEBSITE: www.oceanhousecorpuschristi.com
ROOMS: 5 Suites; Private baths
CHILDREN: Call ahead
PETS: Not allowed; Resident outdoor cat

Ocean House Shrimp

Makes 8 Entrée Servings or 16 Appetizer Servings

*"Your guests will love this typical Texas taste. If you prefer
a spicier flavor, just increase the amount of serrano pepper!"*
—INNKEEPER, *Ocean House*

3 pounds large or extra-large shrimp,
    peeled and deveined
Kosher salt and black pepper, to taste
½ stick (¼ cup) butter
8 serrano chile peppers, chopped (with seeds)
¼ cup red bell pepper, chopped
¼ cup onion, chopped
2 tablespoons fresh garlic, minced
½ cup fresh parsley, chopped
½ cup fresh cilantro, chopped
2 leaves fresh basil, chopped
¼ cup chardonnay wine (or other dry white wine)
Juice of 1 lemon

Sprinkle the shrimp with salt and pepper; set aside. In a large
skillet, melt butter over medium heat. Add serrano peppers, red
bell pepper, onion, garlic, parsley, cilantro, and basil; cook for
2 minutes. Increase heat to medium-high; add shrimp and wine.
Cook for 4–5 minutes more, or until the shrimp turn pink and
are opaque throughout. Drizzle with fresh lemon juice and serve.

AMELIA'S PLACE

In an old factory building constructed in 1924, Amelia's apartment
on the third floor is the only existing apartment in downtown Dallas from the 1920s.

Amelia, a feminist from Louisiana who is said to be the best cook in three parishes, offers genuine Southern hospitality. Guests say that her breakfast is so delicious and so big, you can skip lunch. Amelia also offers a very generous Happy Hour. Books and games galore provide evening entertainment along with a few tunes on a baby grand.

Guests of all persuasions are welcome. Leave your prejudices at the door.

INNKEEPER: Amelia Core Jenkins

ADDRESS: 5425 Gaston Avenue, #112, Dallas, Texas 75214

TELEPHONE: (214) 827-3779

E-MAIL: ameliacorej@sbcglobal.net

WEBSITE: www.ameliasplace.com

ROOMS: 1 Room; Private bath

CHILDREN: Age 14 and older welcome

PETS: Not allowed

Shrimp Bogue Falaya

Makes 8 Servings

*"This dish is named for a river in southeast Louisiana
that flows into Lake Ponchartrain. An Indian name,
Bogue Falaya means 'singing water,'"*
—INNKEEPER, *Amelia's Place Bed & Breakfast*

3 cups water, plus 1 cup water
1½ teaspoons salt
1½ cups uncooked long-grain white rice (do not use instant rice)
2 tablespoons soy sauce
5 chicken bouillon cubes
2 stick (½ cup) butter
2 large ribs celery, sliced crosswise into ⅓-inch crescents
2 bunches green onions (white and green parts), sliced into ⅓-inch pieces
8 ounces whole mushrooms, sliced top to bottom into ⅓-inch slices
1 pound fresh, peeled medium-to-large shrimp
2 teaspoons freshly ground pepper

Preheat oven to 350°F. In a medium saucepan, combine 3 cups of water, salt and rice; bring to a boil. Reduce heat to a low simmer, cover and cook for 18 minutes, or until done. Remove from heat and let stand, covered, for 5–6 minutes. Fluff rice with a fork to keep grains from sticking together.

In a small saucepan, combine 1 cup water, soy sauce, and bouillon. Simmer over medium-low heat until bouillon dissolves (help by mashing bouillon with the back of a spoon). Remove from heat; set aside.

In a large skillet, melt butter over medium heat. Cook celery, mushrooms and onions until mushrooms have wilted. Add shrimp and soy mixture. Cook, stirring constantly, until shrimp turn pink. Remove from heat; add the cooked rice and toss lightly to blend. Stir in the pepper.

Preheat oven to 350°F. Spray the bottom and sides of a large baking dish (such as a 2½-quart deep baking dish or a 9x13-inch baking pan) with nonstick cooking spray. Put the rice/shrimp mixture into the baking dish and bake, covered, for 30 minutes. Serve at once (or lower oven temperature to 180°F and hold for up to an hour or so).

HILL COUNTRY EQUESTRIAN LODGE

Hill Country Equestrian Lodge is located on a 100-year-old cattle ranch in the heart of the Texas Hill Country, an area world renowned for its unique natural beauty and pioneer history. Here, trails cross crystal-clear streams and wind through 6,000 acres of rolling hills dotted with live oak, yucca and wildflowers.

Whitetail deer, turkey, jackrabbits and other wildlife are frequently spotted during rides or from your porch.

For those guests who want to improve their horsemanship skills, Hill Country Equestrian Lodge offers its own 5 or 7 day Whole Horsemanship Clinics. From the ground to the saddle, students learn how to draw upon methods ranging from Join-up to Centered Riding to experience the ultimate horse and rider relationship.

Early Texas-style cabins, built of native limestone and cedar, echo the homes of the sturdy German and Polish immigrants who settled the region in days gone by, while providing guests luxurious sanctuary from the rigors of modern-day life.

INNKEEPERS: Dianne Lindig and Peter Lovett

ADDRESS: 1580 Hay Holler Road, Bandera, Texas 78003

TELEPHONE: (830) 796-7950

E-MAIL: info@hillcountryequestlodge.com

WEBSITE: www.hillcountryequestlodge.com

ROOMS: 5 Rooms; 4 Cottages; Private baths

CHILDREN: Welcome

PETS: Horses okay; Resident dogs, cats & horses

Pete's Pasta

Makes 8 Servings

*Seafood, sausage and vegetables combine
to make a very pretty pasta dish!*

1 (16-ounce) roll breakfast sausage
1 pound raw shrimp, peeled, rinsed and drained
1 (6-ounce) can crab meat, undrained
1 (6½-ounce) can chopped clams in clam juice,
    undrained
1 (12-ounce) bag cherry tomatoes
1 bunch (about 1 pound) fresh broccoli,
    cut into bite-size pieces
1 cup snow peas
1 yellow bell pepper, cut into strips
1 (8-ounce) package sliced mushrooms
2 tablespoons salt, divided
1 (16-ounce) package angel hair pasta
½ cup olive oil
½ teaspoon garlic, chopped, crushed
⅔ cup fresh Parmesan cheese, grated

In a large skillet, cook sausage until done. Drain on paper towels.
Cover with a plate to keep warm. In a large saucepan, combine
shrimp, crab, clams and clam juice. Bring to a boil, lower heat
and simmer, stirring frequently, until shrimp turn pink and are
opaque throughout, about 5 minutes. Remove from heat; cover
and set aside.

In a microwave-safe bowl, combine cherry tomatoes, broccoli, snow
peas, yellow bell pepper, and mushrooms. Cover and microwave
for 5 minutes; leave covered and set aside.

In a large pot, bring 4 quarts of water and 1 tablespoon salt to a
boil. Add pasta and cook for about 3–4 minutes. Drain pasta and
return to pot. Add olive oil, the remaining 1 tablespoon of salt
and garlic; toss to combine.

Divide ingredients equally into 8 bowls in the following order:
pasta, sausage, vegetables, seafood with juice and Parmesan cheese.
Serve immediately.

BED AND BREAKFAST SPA

A calming sanctuary in central Austin, the Bed and Breakfast Spa is a rare find in the wonderful old neighborhood of Tarrytown. Melt your cares away in the patio sauna or steam room. Unwind in the huge indoor heated spa/hot tub with multi-modal therapeutic massage jets. Ease your aching back with a gentle stretch provided by the automatic shiatzu massage table in the East Wing. Divine bed and breakfast guestroom amenities include a massage chair and a foot massager.

All accommodations are extremely spacious at the Bed and Breakfast Spa. The Palace Above is a second story abode with its own entrance, boasts an absolutely dreamy massive brass bed, and has a screened patio surrounded by oak trees. The kitchen nook in each room offers a peaceful space to enjoy a private, leisurely Continental breakfast of fruit, luscious pastries, and fresh juice. There is a complete New York-style kitchen in the guesthouse.

"What a healing environment—romantic, fun, and so central to everything. Check out Umlauf Sculpture Gardens and Zilker Botanical Gardens—you'll be delighted." —GUEST

INNKEEPER: Jule Vigness

ADDRESS: 1309 Meriden Lane, Austin, Texas 78703

TELEPHONE: (512) 499-0081

E-MAIL: jule@bnbspa.com

WEBSITE: www.bnbspa.com

ROOMS: 3 Rooms; 1 Cottage; Private baths

CHILDREN: Unable to accommodate

PETS: Not allowed

Camper's Delight

Makes 3 to 4 Servings

"I came up with this gem while camping on my boat in Oregon. It's a great recipe for the campsite, using ramen noodles, or at home with linguini or thin spaghetti. The sausage and shrimp and creamy tomatoes make this dish quite satisfying on any cool evening."
—MANAGER, *Bed and Breakfast Spa*

10–12 ounces pasta
3 pork, beef or chicken sausage links,
    cut into bite-size pieces
12 shrimp, cut in half
4 medium tomatoes, sliced
2–3 cloves garlic, chopped
½ teaspoon dried basil
¼ teaspoon garlic powder
3–4 ounces cream cheese

In a large pot, boil water for pasta. Put pasta in boiling water while you are preparing the sauce. If you put it in right after you finish browning the sausage and cooking the shrimp; it might be ready just in time to combine with the sauce.

In a large frying pan, brown the sausage stirring to brown on all sides (about 7 minutes). Remove from pan: place in a covered bowl. Add shrimp to the frying pan; cook for 2–3 minutes stirring often. Remove from pan and set aside. Slowly add tomatoes to the frying pan. The tomatoes must sizzle, but don't let the grease smoke. Flip the tomatoes after 5 minutes; add garlic; cook for another 5 minutes, being carefully not to burn the garlic. Chop up the tomatoes with spatula; add basil and garlic powder. Add cream cheese 1 tablespoon at a time; stirring briskly. Add the sausage and shrimp to the tomato sauce. Cook 5 more minutes. Drain the pasta when it is cooked; but do not rinse it. Add pasta to tomato sauce and mix well. Serve.

TIPS:
Season shrimp with salt, pepper, and a nice splash of apple cider vinegar. Substitute dried basil for dill and juice of ½ a lemon for a different flavor.

Desserts

Desserts

*Dessert should
close the meal gently
and not in a
pyrotechnic blaze of glory.*

—ALAN KOEHLER

CRYSTAL RIVER INN

If your travels take you anywhere near Austin or San Antonio, don't miss the Crystal River Inn, one of the oldest and most famous bed and breakfast/country inns in Texas. The inn is located in beautiful San Marcos, one of the crown jewels of the Hill Country. For over twenty years, the Dillon family and Crystal River Inn have been working hard to capture the peace, beauty, and history of this unique chunk of Texas.

Just over two hours from Houston, the bustling little riverside town of San Marcos is surrounded by scenery that is among the best in Texas. San Marcos is home to nature theme parks, world-class shopping, whitewater sports, picturesque historic districts, merry festivals, great antiquing, wineries, theater and fine dining.

If you prefer a more relaxing few days, sleep until noon and have breakfast in bed. Rock the afternoon away on the veranda. Join new friends for a sumptuous brunch.

INNKEEPERS:	Mike, Cathy and Sarah Dillon
ADDRESS:	326 West Hopkins, San Marcos, Texas 78666
TELEPHONE:	(512) 396-3739; (888) 396-3739
E-MAIL:	info@crystalriverinn.com
WEBSITE:	www.crystalriverinn.com
ROOMS:	12 Rooms; 3 Suites; Private baths
CHILDREN:	Welcome
PETS:	Call ahead

Caramelized Upside-Down Bread Pudding

Makes 6 to 8 Servings

"This heavenly concoction is a variation on make-ahead
baked French toast. It is a cross between sticky buns
and fluffy custard – fabulous for special brunches."
This dish needs to be started the night before serving.
—INNKEEPER, *Crystal River Inn.*

1½ sticks (¾ cup) butter, melted
2 cups brown sugar, packed
½ teaspoon cinnamon
½ cup raisins (or chopped almonds)
6–8 slices (1½–2 inches thick) French or Italian bread
6 eggs
2 cups milk
1½ teaspoons vanilla extract
½ teaspoon ground nutmeg
Maple syrup, for serving (optional)

Combine melted butter, brown sugar and cinnamon; spread evenly into the bottom of a 9x13-inch baking dish. Sprinkle with raisins or almonds. Lay slices of bread on top (slices may be trimmed or squeezed slightly to fit the dish, if necessary). In a small bowl, whisk together eggs, milk, vanilla and nutmeg; pour evenly over the bread. Cover and refrigerate overnight.

The next morning, preheat oven to 350°F. Bake for 35–40 minutes, or until puffed and golden. Serve pieces of the pudding with the syrup from the bottom of the baking dish spooned over the top of each portion. Maple syrup is usually not necessary, but may be offered on the side.

HOLLY HILL
HOMESTEAD & RETREAT

"A special place with special food for special people"

The hills of northeast Texas are home to the farm-style Holly Hill Homestead and Retreat. The accommodations at the bed and breakfast are cozy, informal, and charming, and the view from the sun porch is absolutely awe-inspiring.

Country gourmet meals are prepared at Holly Hill and the food is always fresh and made from scratch. The ambiance for casual dining in the large kitchen is enhanced by the wood cook stove and open fireplace. Private dining on one of the porches or outdoors can also be arranged. New recipes are tested by the innkeeper for the regular Wednesday luncheon. It begins at noon and ends when the food runs out. Reservations are requested for the folks interested in taking part in the Wednesday taste tests.

Garden tours are offered during every season of the year at Holly Hill Homestead. Small groups may participate in gardening and cooking workshops held at the inn on a regular basis. A workshop schedule is listed on the events page of the bed and breakfast website.

INNKEEPERS: Tim and Jolene Wilson

ADDRESS: 9076 Texas Highway 11, Hughes Springs, Texas 75656

TELEPHONE: (903) 639-1318

E-MAIL: jolene@hollyhillhomestead.com

WEBSITE: www.hollyhillhomestead.com

ROOMS: 2 Rooms; Private baths

CHILDREN: Age 12 and older welcome

PETS: Not allowed

Chocolate Bread Pudding

Makes 9 to 12 Servings

*"The recipe calls for one loaf of French bread, cubed,
crust left on, but you may not need the whole loaf.
Bread pudding is intended as a use for stale bread.
I often use pieces of this or that, muffins, and croissants."*
—INNKEEPER, *Holly Hill*

¾ cup good quality unsweetened cocoa
1¾ cup sugar
2 cups whole milk
1 cup half-and-half.
3 eggs
½ teaspoon salt
1 tablespoon vanilla
1 loaf of French bread, cubed, with crust left on.
½ cup pecans, chopped
¼ cup butter

In a medium saucepan, mix the cocoa and sugar; whisk in milk and half-and-half. Stir over medium heat until steaming. Set aside to cool.

Preheat oven to 350°F. Spray a 9x13-inch pan with nonstick spray and dust with a touch of cocoa. In a small bowl, combine eggs, salt, and vanilla; beat well. Add a single layer of bread cubes to the bottom of the pan. Spoon a layer of chocolate sauce over the bread. Drizzle the egg mixture over the bread. Repeat layer of bread cubes and chocolate sauce. (Do not use more bread than the liquid will absorb). Press bread down with a spoon so cubes will be saturated with liquid. Sprinkle with nuts and dot with butter.

You may cover and refrigerate at this point.

Bake uncovered for 40–45 minutes until set in the middle and a knife comes out clean. Do not over bake. To serve, top with whipped cream and your choice of sauce. In the South, bread pudding comes with a traditional whisky sauce, or you can use a caramel, mocha, or Melba sauce—or just fresh strawberries and raspberries.

VARIATIONS FOR LOW-FAT:
For a low-fat version of this recipe, substitute 3 cups of skim milk for the cream and milk; use ¾ cup of an egg white product in place of eggs, and eliminate the butter.

GREAT OAKS MANOR

Massive Corinthian columns flank the front porch steps of this three-story Sugar Land and Houston area bed and breakfast called Great Oaks Manor. Civil War hero Clement Newton Bassett incorporated resplendent period architectural details into the design when he built his stunning Greek Revival residence that now serves as an impressive inn. The majestic carved oak staircase is accented with stained-glass windows that shine into the stately foyer. There are eight fireplaces with the original wood or marble mantles, which provide authentic ambience in this mansion steeped in colorful Texas history.

The two-acre grounds where century-old oaks create a shady canopy are a natural invitation to take a nap in the old-fashioned hammock. A lavish breakfast buffet is served daily in the elegant dining room or on the verandah. Murder mystery weekends are scheduled regularly at the Great Oaks Manor and feature a pirate feast proceeding the murder and mayhem.

INNKEEPERS:	Carey and Fred Gulliksen
ADDRESS:	419 Macek Road, Richmond, Texas 77469
TELEPHONE:	(281) 343-9551
E-MAIL:	info@greatoaksmanor.com
WEBSITE:	www.GreatOaksManor.com
ROOMS:	6 Rooms; Private baths
CHILDREN:	Age 12 and older welcome
PETS:	Not allowed; Resident dogs, cats, and many chickens and ducks

Miss Georgia's
Southern Bread Pudding

Makes 9 to 12 Servings

"Miss Georgia was an old woman who lived 'on the wrong side of the tracks' from my grandparent's house, where I spent most of my childhood summers. I would sneak around the block and down her street on the pretext of going to the Woolworth's which was in the opposite direction! She would serve me the best bread pudding I was ever to taste, until I finally recreated her recipe, 50 years later."
—INNKEEPER, *Great Oaks Manor*

1 loaf of French bread,
    cut into cubes to make 9 cups
4 large eggs
4 cups half-and-half
½ teaspoon nutmeg
¼ teaspoon cinnamon
½ cup butter, melted (preferably European style)
¼ cup light brown sugar, packed
2 teaspoons good Bourbon Vanilla
½ cup peaches, diced to about
    ½-inch piece, and preferably fresh

SAUCE:
½ cup butter
1 cup light brown sugar, packed
2 teaspoons cornstarch
½ cup whipping cream
¼ cup Peach Brandy

Preheat oven to 325°F. Butter a 9x9-inch baking pan. Place bread cubes in baking pan. In a large bowl, beat eggs with a whisk; add all remaining ingredients, with the exception of the sauce ingredients. Mix well. Pour over the bread and stir. Bake for 40–45 minutes until a knife inserted in the center, comes out almost clean.

For the sauce: In a small saucepan, combine butter and brown sugar. Boil for 1 minute. Remove from the heat. In a small bowl, add cornstarch to the whipping cream; combine and add to the saucepan. Heat through again until sugar is dissolved and mixture is slightly thickened. Stir in Peach Brandy. Keep warm as a side to the bread pudding. Can be refrigerated and reheated.

SEVEN GABLES

"Make way for a new kind of Christian retreat.
Experience God in our small town and quiet setting." —INNKEEPER

A stay at Seven Gables will provide you the opportunity to enjoy your morning on the wrap around porch as the sun comes up. There you will find a peaceful swing and comfy porch furniture, while sipping your first cup of freshly brewed gourmet coffee.

Delight in tastefully decorated rooms with carefully selected and placed accessories. An array of bath and body products are provided for your enjoyment, along with thick, fluffy towels and monogrammed robes. Dessert is served in the evening, if you aren't out taking in the sights.

If you require directions to restaurants or area attractions, you can count on your hostess to provide guidance for endless hours of enjoyment in Mount Vernon. While visiting, browse our antique, gift, and retail shops in town for the perfect item to remember your stay.

INNKEEPER: Debi Renner

ADDRESS: 318 South Kaufman Street, Mt Vernon, Texas 75457

TELEPHONE: (903) 537-3391

E-MAIL: TheInnkeeperBB@aol.com

WEBSITE: www.mtvernontexas.com

ROOMS: 1 Room; 1 Suite; Private baths

CHILDREN: Age 13 and older welcome

PETS: Not allowed; Resident cat and dog

Bread Pudding With a Twist

Makes 10 to 12 Servings

4½ cups milk
½ cup butter, divided in half
6 eggs
1 cup sugar
1 cup brown sugar
2 teaspoons cinnamon
1 loaf of sliced bread
2 apples, cored, and thinly sliced
1 cup raisins

ICING:
1 cup powdered sugar
1 teaspoon vanilla
1 teaspoon cinnamon
Milk to moisten

Preheat oven to 350°F. Grease a 9x13-inch baking pan with nonstick cooking spray.

In a large saucepan, combine milk and ¼ cup of butter; bring to a simmer, slowly, being careful not to scorch the milk. Remove from heat; set aside. In a large bowl, combine eggs, sugar, and cinnamon; whisk thoroughly. Slowly pour the heated milk and butter into the egg mixture; whisking until fully blended.

Spread half of the bread cubes in the bottom of the baking pan. Layer the apples, followed by the raisins on top of the bread. Top with the remaining bread cubes. Pour the egg and milk mixture over the bread a bit at a time, allowing the liquid to be absorbed. Cover the bread pudding with foil; place on the top rack of the oven; bake for 50–60 minutes.

For the icing: In a small bowl, combine sugar, vanilla, cinnamon, and enough milk to make a thin consistency for drizzling. Set aside.

When Bread Pudding has finished baking, drizzle the icing on top, and serve warm.

THE LODGES
AT LOST MAPLES

From the sound of gentle breezes rustling the leaves to the breathtaking views, the Lodges at Lost Maples is truly the ultimate Hill Country retreat. The inn is located in an area known as the "Swiss Alps of Texas." The rugged terrain and elevations as high as 2,100 feet above sea level make this area popular with recreational motorcyclists and bicyclists, as well as those who enjoy sightseeing.

The Sweetheart Suite offers the perfect romantic getaway with a king size bed and two- person Jacuzzi whirlpool bathtub. Guest robes and incredible views are the extra details that make any occasion a special one.

"We loved your cabin. It was far more than we expected. Watching the birds in the feeder was a real treat. We'll be back for a sky tour and more of your wonderful breakfasts." —GUEST

INNKEEPERS:	The Hathorn Family
ADDRESS:	Ranch Road 337, Vanderpool, Texas 78885
MAILING:	(PO Box 215) 78885
TELEPHONE:	(830) 966-5178; (877) 216-5627; (830) 966-5179 fax
E-MAIL:	lodges@lostmaplescabins.com
WEBSITE:	www.lostmaplescabins.com
ROOMS:	5 Cabins; Private baths
CHILDREN:	Welcome
PETS:	Not allowed

The Lodges's Rustic Chocolate Bread Pudding

Makes 12 Servings

*"These are individual servings of chocolate bread pudding
with a warm surprise in the center."*
—Innkeeper, *The Lodges at Lost Maples*

2 tablespoons butter
½ cup milk chocolate chips
½ cup brown sugar, packed
2 eggs, slightly beaten
¼ teaspoon cinnamon
½ teaspoon vanilla extract
1½ cups heavy cream
½ cup milk
3 cups day-old bread crumbs
3 (1-ounce) squares dark or semisweet chocolate
Powdered sugar, for garnish

Preheat oven to 350°F. Spray 12 muffin cups with nonstick cooking spray. In a microwave-safe bowl, melt butter and chocolate chips together in the microwave; stir well to combine. Whisk the brown sugar into the butter mixture. Add eggs, cinnamon and vanilla; whisk until well blended. Add cream and milk; whisk until well blended. Gently fold in bread cubes until combined; let stand for 10–15 minutes to allow the mixture to absorb most of the liquid.

Divide the bread pudding mixture between the muffin cups. Cut each square of chocolate into 4 pieces. Push one chocolate piece into the middle of the mixture in each muffin cup.

Bake for 35 minutes, or until the bread pudding is set. Remove from the muffin cups and place in paper muffin liners, if desired, to serve. Serve warm, sprinkled with powdered sugar.

1110 CARRIAGE HOUSE INN

The Carriage House Inn is close to historic downtown Austin and a short walk from the University of Texas. This two-story Colonial home is graced with many windows and accented by stately trees. An expansive deck, a pagoda gazebo, and a koi pond with a waterfall complete the idyllic setting. The interior of the inn features hardwood floors, antique tile, and a friendly ghost. Lava rock from a volcano in the area was used to build the guesthouse on the property. Fresh flowers adorn each room, each suite, and the cottages.

The full breakfast served at the Carriage House has been selected as one of the top ten best country breakfasts in the United States. Guests enjoy their own table as they savor the fresh, and often organic, morning meal. The menu changes daily and may include homemade waffles, scones, and biscuits.

INNKEEPER: Tressie Damron

ADDRESS: 1110 West 22½ Street, Austin, Texas

TELEPHONE: (512) 472-2333; (866) 472-2333; (512) 476-0218 fax

E-MAIL: dcarriagehouse@aol.com

WEBSITE: www.carriagehouseinn.org

ROOMS: 7 Rooms; 3 Suites; 2 Cottages; Private baths

CHILDREN: Age 16 and older welcome

PETS: Not allowed

Berry Pudding Torte

Makes 8 to 10 Servings

*"We usually serve this with
homemade whipping cream and a small cookie."*
—INNKEEPER, *1110 Carriage House*

2 cups cold milk
¾ cup granulated sugar
¼ cup flour
1 egg, beaten
1½ teaspoons vanilla extract
1 cup fresh strawberries, washed,
   sliced lengthwise
1 cup fresh blueberries, washed
Fresh mint, to garnish

In a medium saucepan, heat milk just until it begins to bubble around the edges. Turn heat to low. In a small bowl, combine sugar and flour; stir into milk mixture; add the egg; cook until mixture is thick. Turn off heat; stir in vanilla extract.

Let pudding cool only slightly. Pour warm pudding into small individual heatproof serving bowls; top with strawberries, blueberries, and a mint sprig. Serve.

THE ANGLIN ROSE

Nestled among centuries-old oak trees in the town of Cleburne, The Anglin Rose has recently been restored to its original 1892 elegance. This painted lady Victorian features three fireplaces, an octagonal second-floor turret, and an original stained-glass keyhole window. Within an hours drive of Dallas and thirty minutes from Ft. Worth, this residence was built for John Luther and Annie

Cleveland, owners of Cleburne Cottonseed Oil Mill and the Cleveland Hardware store. Mr. Cleveland was instrumental in bringing the railroad to Cleburne.

Select Uncle Sam's room or Grandma's room for your overnight stay. An attic playroom filled with Victorian-era toys awaits you in Uncle Sam's room. Grandma's room is extra large and includes a sitting room and a king-size bed covered with a handmade yoyo quilt.

The magical atmosphere and intimate setting at the Anglin Rose are available for wedding parties. There are three romantic packages from which to choose.

INNKEEPER: Saundra Williams

ADDRESS: 808 South Anglin Street, Cleburne, Texas 76031

TELEPHONE: (817) 641-7433

E-MAIL: anglinrose@htcomp.net

WEBSITE: www.users.htcomp.net/anglinrose

ROOMS: 2 Rooms; Private baths; one located across the hall

CHILDREN: Unable to accommodate

PETS: Not allowed

Chocolate Pecan Pie

Makes 6 to 8 Servings

"Always a hit at luncheons and parties."
—INNKEEPER, *Anglin Rose*

1 stick of butter, melted
3 eggs, beaten
½ cup flour
1 can evaporated milk
3 cups sugar
3 teaspoons cocoa
1 teaspoon vanilla
Dash of salt
2 cups of pecans
2 (9-inch) prepared piecrusts

Preheat oven to 350°F. In a medium bowl, start with melted butter and add each of the next 8 ingredients, one at a time; mixing well after each. Pour into 2 prepared piecrusts. Bake for 30–35 minutes or until done.

GRUENE APPLE

Escape the pressures of everyday life and relax in the privacy of the Gruene Apple's gracious atmosphere. The inn boasts 14 spectacular theme rooms designed to provide an experience of total luxury. The creations of many artists and craftsmen have made each room a special retreat. The inn is filled with items collected by Linda and Lloyd over their 43 years of marriage and travels.

When you wake in the morning make your way to the dining room with its French doors opening to the tile patio, and linger over a gourmet breakfast at which guests are invited to choose from new specialty items everyday.

INNKEEPERS: Ki, Lloyd and Linda Kleypas
ADDRESS: 1235 Gruene Road, New Braunfels, Texas 78130
TELEPHONE: (830) 643-1234
E-MAIL: info@grueneapple.com
WEBSITE: www.grueneapple.com
ROOMS: 14 Rooms; Private baths
CHILDREN: Unable to accommodate
PETS: Not allowed; Resident cats

Apple Cream Cheese Tart

Makes 12 to 14 Servings

CRUST:
1 stick (½ cup) butter, room temperature
$^1/_3$ cup sugar
¼ teaspoon vanilla extract
1 cup flour

FILLLING:
1 (8-ounce) package cream cheese,
    room temperature
¼ cup plus $^1/_3$ cup sugar
1 egg
½ teaspoon vanilla extract
1½ teaspoons cinnamon
6 cups Granny Smith apples, peeled and sliced
¼ cup slivered almonds

For the crust: Preheat oven to 450°F. In a small bowl, cream together butter, ⅓ cup sugar and vanilla. Blend in the flour. Pat dough into the bottom and 1 inch up the sides of an ungreased 9-inch pie pan.

For the filling: In a small bowl, combine cream cheese and ¼ cup sugar. Add egg and vanilla; beat until smooth. Pour into the pie pan. In a large bowl, combine cinnamon and ⅓ cups sugar. Add sliced apples; toss to coat. Arrange apples over cream cheese mixture. Sprinkle with almonds.

Bake for 10 minutes. Lower oven temperature to 400°F; bake for 35 minutes more, or until apples are tender. Let cool in pan on a wire rack. Slice and serve warm or chilled. Store the tart in the refrigerator.

MURSKI HOMESTEAD

"It ain't bragging if it's a fact!"

—Voted *"Best Weekend Escape"* by *Inn Traveler* magazine

The Murski homestead, was the original cotton farm built in the 1880s by the great-great- grandparents of the husband of the innkeeper. Today the visitor is pampered with the amenities of luxury while enjoying the quiet simplicity of country life. Relax in the evening on the century-old front porch and listen to the sounds of wildlife.

There are three beautiful rooms to choose from all named after herbs: the Lavender Room, the Sage Room, and the Rosemary Room—all with private baths and wonderfully comfortable beds with luxurious bed linens.

The Murskis also host cooking classes. Refer to their website for an up-to-date schedule.

INNKEEPER:	Pamela Murski
ADDRESS:	1662 Old Independence Road, Brenham, Texas 77833
TELEPHONE:	(979) 830-1021; (877) 690-0676
E-MAIL:	pmurski@sbcglobal.net
WEBSITE:	www.murskihomesteadbb.com
ROOMS:	3 Rooms; Private baths
CHILDREN:	Age 10 and older welcome
PETS:	Not allowed; Resident cats, a dog, donkeys and Longhorn

Grandmother McGlaun's Strawberry Shortcake

Make 4 to 6 Servings

"My paternal grandmother created this recipe when trying to duplicate a shortcake she had eaten in a restaurant. The restaurant would not share the recipe with her."
—INNKEEPER, *Murski Homestead*

¼ teaspoon salt
2 teaspoons fresh baking powder
1 cup white flour
½ cup whole milk
¼ cup butter, melted
1 pound or more fresh strawberries
½–1 cup sugar, depending on
    desired sweetness of strawberries

WHIPPED TOPPING:
Heavy cream, whipped
3–4 tablespoons sugar
vanilla

Preheat oven to 475°F. In a medium bowl, combine salt, baking powder, and flour; add milk; stir well. Pour in melted butter; stir until blended. Divide dough between 2 pie pans; pat down into base of each pan. Bake for 14–18 minutes or until golden. Remove from oven; let cool.

Wash, hull and slice strawberries. In a large bowl, toss together the strawberries and sugar, coating all the strawberries. Cover strawberries and let macerate to develop juices; at least 1 hour. Whip heavy cream until peaks form. Add a 3–4 tablespoons sugar and 1 teaspoon vanilla to the whipped cream. Mix and set aside.

Divide strawberries in half between the two shortcakes. Top with whipped cream. Slice in wedges to serve. Garnish with a fresh cut organic rose.

TIPS:
Sometimes I macerate my strawberries with a homemade herbal liqueur as well as sugar. You can also mix in a tablespoon of chopped sweet herbs to the shortcake dough before

THE QUEEN ANNE

Breakfast at the Queen Anne is a wonderful dining experience and is served on antique china accompanied by candlelight and soft music. Guests enjoy a full gourmet breakfast including home-made breads, jams, jellies, praline sauce and many house specialties.

The sideboard in the dining room is laid ready for hot tea any time of the day with select Ashby's teas, fine teacups, and a biscuit barrel filled with delicate cookies.

"What a romantic interlude you provide weary travelers. We love your house and will be telling everyone on our journey. Breakfast is a marvelous respite from restaurant fare. " —GUEST

INNKEEPERS:	Beth and George Ibarra
ADDRESS:	1915 Sealy Avenue, Galveston, Texas 77550
TELEPHONE:	(409) 763-7088; (888) 763-7088
E-MAIL:	stay@galvestonqueenanne.com
WEBSITE:	www.galvestonqueenanne.com
ROOMS:	5 Rooms; 1 Suite; Private baths
CHILDREN:	Age 12 and older welcome
PETS:	Not allowed

Lemon Cake

Makes 16 Servings

Be sure to notice that the oven temperature is lowered two times during baking. The cake bakes for a total of 45 minutes.

CAKE:
1 box Duncan Hines Lemon Supreme cake mix
¾ cup vegetable oil
1 cup apricot nectar
4 eggs

GLAZE:
Juice and grated zest of 2 lemons
2 cups powdered sugar

For the cake: Preheat oven to 350°F. Spray a 12-cup Bundt pan or tube pan with nonstick cooking spray. In a large bowl, combine cake mix, oil and apricot nectar; beat well. Add eggs, one at a time, beating after each addition. Pour batter into pan.

Bake for 15 minutes. Lower oven temperature to 325°F and bake for 15 more minutes. Lower oven temperature to 300°F and bake for 15 more minutes. Let cake cool for 20 minutes in the pan on a wire rack.

For the glaze: While the cake is cooling, make the glaze by combining the juice and zest of the lemons with the powdered sugar. Stir until smooth.

Turn the cake out onto a cake plate. Spoon the lemon glaze over the cake while it is still warm. Let cake cool completely before slicing and serving.

Camp David

Conveniently located on far west Main Street, Camp David offers a charming collection of five cottages behind the main house. As with the original "Camp David," each cottage is named for a local tree. Fredericksburg boasts several award-winnng wineries that you may visit to learn a bit about the art of winemaking and sample their wines.

"Thank you for an extremely enjoyable stay. Breakfast was scrumptious and your hospitality was engaging." —Guest

INNKEEPERS:	Molly and Bob Sagebiel
ADDRESS:	708 West Main, Fredericksburg, Texas 78624
TELEPHONE:	(830) 997-7797; (866) 427-8374
E-MAIL:	campdavidbb@austin.rr.com
WEBSITE:	www.campdavidbb.com
ROOMS:	1 Suite; 5 Cottages; Private baths
CHILDREN:	Age 12 and older welcome
PETS:	Not allowed

Ann's Luscious Lime Pound Cake

Makes 16 to 24 Servings

*"Ann is our daughter. She loves the taste of lime
and is partial to white chocolate."*
—INNKEEPER, *Camp David Bed & Breakfast*

1 cup white chocolate chips (such as Ghirardelli)
2 sticks (1 cup) butter, room temperature
1½ cups sugar
2 teaspoons vanilla extract
3 large or extra-large eggs
3 tablespoons grated lime zest (from about 3 large limes)
2½ cups flour
1 teaspoon baking powder
½ teaspoon salt
1⅓ cups buttermilk
3 tablespoons fresh lime juice
1 cup powdered sugar

Preheat oven to 350°F. Grease and flour 4 3¼x6-inch mini-loaf pans or a 12-cup capacity Bundt pan. Put chips in a microwave-safe bowl. Heat for 1 minute in the microwave. Stir, then microwave for 10–20 seconds at a time, stirring and melting until smooth; set aside.

In a large bowl, cream together butter, sugar, and vanilla. Beat in eggs, one at a time, beating well after each addition. Beat in lime zest and melted chips. In a separate bowl, sift together flour, baking powder, and salt. Beat flour mixture into batter alternately with buttermilk, beginning and ending with the flour mixture, beating well after each addition. Spoon batter into pan(s).

Bake mini-loaves for 25–35 minutes; Bundt cake for 45–55 minutes, or until a toothpick inserted in the center comes out clean. Cool in pan(s) on a wire rack (10 minutes for mini-loaves or 20 minutes for Bundt cake).

Make a glaze by combining lime juice and powdered sugar; stir until smooth. Remove warm cake from pan(s). Poke holes in cake(s) with a toothpick; drizzle with ½ of the glaze. Wait for 5 minutes, repeat with the remaining glaze. Cool completely before serving. This cake freezes well.

HOLEKAMP HOUSE

"A Gem in the Texas Hill Country"

The town of Comfort is an antique shopper's paradise and the HoleKamp House serves as an excellent base-camp for treasure hunters. This 1910 Sears and Roebuck kit home is five blocks from historic downtown Comfort. The house has plenty of history and the generous innkeepers have many books and photos to share that relate to their old Sears Mansion.

Sleep each evening under crisp, sweet-smelling linens in one of the four rooms or in the cabin. Aunt Dolly's bright, cheerful room contains a twelve-foot-long, built-in window seat creating an invitation to sit, relax, and enjoy the morning sunshine. The rustic, spacious cedar cabin has a kitchenette, large sitting area, and all of the comforts of home.

For your breakfast-time pleasure, the inn's rosemary eggs are superb. The evening dessert hour is extremely popular with over-night visitors. In the words of one guest, *"The desserts are to die for."* Kerrville State Park is just a few minutes away from HoleKamp House. The park trails are a great place to walk off some of those dessert calories.

INNKEEPERS:	John and Mary Straley
ADDRESS:	610 Second Street, Comfort, Texas 78013
TELEPHONE:	(830) 995-5554; (877) 859-9946
E-MAIL:	stay@holekamphouse.com
WEBSITE:	www.holekamphouse.com
ROOMS:	4 Rooms; 1 Suite; 1 Cottage; Private baths
CHILDREN:	Age 12 and older welcome
PETS:	Not allowed; Resident cats and a dog

Cream Cheese Pound Cake

Makes 6 to 8 Servings

1 (8-ounce) package cream cheese, softened
½ cup butter, softened
3 cups granulated sugar
6 eggs
3 cups all-purpose flour
2 teaspoons vanilla
1 teaspoon lemon extract

Preheat oven to 325°F. Grease a 10-inch tube pan or Bundt pan with nonstick cooking spray. In a medium bowl, blend cream cheese and butter until smooth; add sugar gradually and beat until fluffy. Add eggs one at a time; beating well after each. Add flour; mix in well. Add vanilla and lemon extract. Mix throughout batter. Pour into prepared pan. Bake for 1 hour and 20 minutes, or until a toothpick inserted in the middle comes out clean.

Fruited Pound Cake Topping

Makes 2 Servings

This dessert can be easily multiplied for more servings.

2 cups of fresh fruit, your choice,
  (peaches, strawberries, blueberries, etc
Sugar, a few tablespoons, to taste
Grand Marnier, a few tablespoons, to taste
2–4 tablespoons Lemon curd, to spread
2 scoops vanilla ice cream, for topping

Marinate fruit in sugar and Grand Marnier for 15 minutes or so. Toast a slice of pound cake. Spread 1–2 tablespoons of lemon curd on toasted cake. Serve with a scoop of ice cream and marinated fruit on the top.

Amaretto Divine

Makes 12 Servings

1 (18.25-ounce) yellow cake mix
2 cups nondairy amaretto creamer, divided
1¼ cups amaretto liqueur, divided
3 eggs
⅓ cup oil
1 (3.5-ounce) instant vanilla pudding
2 cups heavy whipped cream
5–6 ounces chocolate toffee chips
1 chocolate bar, melted
¼–½ cup sliced almonds

Preheat oven to 325°F. Lightly grease 2 8-inch round cake pans with nonstick cooking spray.

In a large bowl, combine cake mix, 1 cup amaretto creamer, 1 cup amaretto liqueur, eggs and oil. Mix until blended well. Pour batter evenly between the 2 cake pans. Bake for 25 minutes. Do not over bake. Allow to cool completely.

In a medium bowl, combine dry pudding mix, 1 cup amaretto creamer, and ¼ cup liqueur. Set aside for 5 minutes until thickened. Whip heavy cream until it forms peaks. Fold whipped cream into amaretto mixture; stir in toffee bits.

Remove cake from cake pans. Spread whipped cream filling on top of bottom layer. Place top cake layer on bottom layer and continue to frost top of cake with the whipped filling. Drizzle cake with melted candy bar; sprinkle with almonds.

VIEH'S BED AND BREAKFAST

The innkeepers at Vieh's also operate Custom Outings, which offers guided adventures in Mexico, including antique shopping in colonial Mexico, birding in the Sierra Madres, butterflying from the high desert to the low coastal plains, palm and plant trips, and general exploring and sea shelling on remote beaches.

Vieh's is a traditional bed and breakfast with genuine Texas hospitality.

INNKEEPERS:	Lana and Charles Vieh
ADDRESS:	18413 Landrum Park Road, San Benito, Texas 78586
TELEPHONE:	(956) 425-4651
E-MAIL:	viehbb@aol.com
WEBSITE:	www.vieh.com
ROOMS:	4 Rooms; 1 Cottage; Private and shared baths
CHILDREN:	Welcome
PETS:	Welcome; call head; Resident parrots and horses

Vieh's Brownies

Makes 9 Brownies

"My grandfather and father owned Vieh's Bakery – '
Makers and bakers of good things to eat' – in Memphis, Tennessee,
in the early 1930's. They developed lots of great recipes,
such as these brownies, which are great served with
the hot fudge sauce and Texas' Blue Bell Ice Cream."
—INNKEEPER, *Vieh's Bed & Breakfast*

½ cup flour
1 cup sugar
4 tablespoons unsweetened cocoa powder
½ teaspoon salt
¼ cup canola oil
2 eggs
1 teaspoon vanilla extract
½ cup chopped pecans
Hot fudge sauce, for serving (optional)
(recipe follows)
Ice cream, for serving (optional)

Preheat oven to 350°F. Butter a 9x9-inch glass-baking dish. In a medium bowl, sift flour, sugar, cocoa powder and salt. Add oil, eggs and vanilla; mix well. Stir in pecans. Pour mixture into baking dish.

Bake for 25 minutes, or until a toothpick inserted in the center comes out clean. To slice, dip a knife into a glass of ice water, wipe knife dry and cut. Serve with hot fudge sauce and ice cream, if desired.

HOT FUDGE SAUCE:
½ cup unsweetened cocoa powder
2 cups sugar
Pinch of salt
⅔ cup milk
2 tablespoons butter
1 teaspoon vanilla extract

In a heavy 2-quart saucepan, mix all of the sauce ingredients, except the vanilla. Bring to a boil over medium heat and let boil, without stirring, for 6 minutes. Remove from heat; stir in vanilla. Serve hot.

OLD MULBERRY INN

Built in the style of a northern Louisiana plantation, the Old Mulberry Inn is a stunning combination of twenty-first-century comforts and nineteenth-century charm. The owners chose an architectural style that represents the antebellum heyday of Jefferson, culling antique shops and salvage yards to furnish the stately Greek Revival inn.

Old Mulberry Inn has been featured in Southern Living, the L.A. Times Magazine, and the travel sections of major Texas newspapers. "This classy five-room inn stands apart," wrote travel editor Harry Shattuck in a Houston Chronicle story featuring just three inns in the state.

The gourmet breakfasts undoubtedly add to this stellar reputation. Signature dishes include Baked Pears with Cranberries, California Artichoke Quiche, Rocky Mountain Grits, and Mulberry Almond Coffeecake.

INNKEEPERS: Donald and Gloria Degn

ADDRESS: 209 East Jefferson Street, Jefferson, Texas 75657

TELEPHONE: (903) 665-1945

E-MAIL: mulberry3@charter.net

WEBSITE: www.oldmulberryinn.com

ROOMS: 5 Rooms; Private baths

CHILDREN: Age 15 and older welcome

PETS: Not allowed

East Texas Cowboy Cookies

Makes 6 Dozen Cookies

2 sticks (1 cup) butter, room temperature
½ cup white sugar
1½ cups brown sugar
2 eggs
1½ teaspoons vanilla extract
2 cups flour
½ teaspoon salt
1 teaspoon baking soda
2 cups old-fashioned rolled oats
   (not quick-cooking oats)
1 (12-ounce) package chocolate chips
   (about 2 cups)
2 cups shredded coconut

Preheat oven to 350°F. Spray a baking sheet with nonstick cooking spray. In a large bowl, cream together butter, white sugar and brown sugar. Beat in eggs and vanilla. Sift together flour, salt and baking soda; add to butter mixture and blend well. Stir in oats, chocolate chips and coconut; mix well.

Drop dough by rounded tablespoonfuls onto the baking sheet. Bake for 12–15 minutes. Cool on the baking sheet for 1 minute, then remove cookies to a wire rack to finish cooling.

Cookies are made of butter and love.

—Anonymous

THE AUSTIN FOLK HOUSE

The closest little hotel to the University of Texas is just two blocks west of the campus and sports its very own parking lot. The Austin Folk House was built in 1880, has been completely restored, has a south facing front porch, and a view of the Texas State Capitol building through a window in the upstairs sitting area. The house is light and airy and the decor is an original blend of antiques and whimsical folk art. Nine rooms comprise the lodging choices at the Austin Folk House, including one room with an external entrance for extra privacy. A long, upstairs hallway serves as a gallery for an extensive collection of folk art paintings.

The hot and delicious Texas-size breakfast buffet is a daily event at Austin Folk House. The heavenly fare may include banana enchiladas, raspberry waffles, gingerbread pancakes with caramelized pecans, egg blossoms, green chile casserole, lots of fresh fruit, homemade biscotti, and a variety of breads.

INNKEEPERS: Sylvia and Chris Mackey

ADDRESS: 506 West 22nd Street, Austin, Texas 78705

TELEPHONE: (512) 472-6700; (866) 472-6700

E-MAIL: sylvia@austinfolkhouse.com

WEBSITE: www.austinfolkhouse.com

ROOMS: 9 Rooms; Private baths

CHILDREN: Age 12 and older welcome

PETS: Not allowed

Thick and Chewy Chocolate Chip Cookies

Makes about 40 Cookies

4¼ cups all-purpose flour
1 teaspoon baking soda
1 teaspoon salt
3 sticks unsalted butter, melted and cool until warm
2 cups light or dark brown sugar, packed
1 cup granulated sugar
2 large eggs plus 2 egg yolks
4 teaspoons vanilla extract
3 cups semisweet chocolate chips

Preheat oven to 325°F. Grease a cookie sheet with nonstick cooking spray.

In a medium bowl, whisk flour, baking soda, and salt; blending well. In a large bowl, beat butter and sugars until thoroughly blended. Beat in eggs, yolks, and vanilla until combined. Add dry ingredients; beat with mixer at low speed until just combined. Stir in chips.

Roll rounded tablespoonfuls of dough into balls. Holding dough ball in fingertips of both hands, pull into two equal halves. Rotate halves 90°s and with jagged surfaces facing up, join halves together at their sides, being careful not to smooth dough's uneven surface. Place formed dough onto cookie sheet, leaving 2½ inches between each ball.

Bake for 6 minutes; rotate baking sheet. Bake for an additional 5–6 minutes, until cookies are light golden brown, and outer edges start to harden. Centers should still be soft and puffy.

Cool cookies on sheets for 2 minutes. Transfer to racks to cool completely.

POMEGRANATE HOUSE

Pomegranate House is a uniquely restored, 1906 country Victorian home where guests can relax and enjoy the atmosphere of a bygone era. Surrounded by magnificent live oaks and arrayed with brilliant seasonal flowers, Pomegranate House is the perfect escape from everyday life.

Enjoy a special romantic getaway package in one of the beautiful Victorian guest rooms. Your weekend will include flowers in your room, a carriage ride to the town square and two tickets to Granbury Live or Granbury Opera House.

INNKEEPERS: Betty and Tommy Potts

ADDRESS: 1002 West Pearl Street, Granbury, Texas 76048

TELEPHONE: (817) 279-7412; (888) 503-7659

E-MAIL: pomegranatehousebandb@yahoo.com

WEBSITE: www.pomhouse.com

ROOMS: 1 Room; 1 Suite; 3 Cottages; Private baths

CHILDREN: Age 12 and older welcome

PETS: Not allowed; Resident dogs

Sweetie Cookies

Makes 6 Dozen Cookies

"These beautiful pink cookies are very popular with our guests.
We serve them daily at our B&B."
—INNKEEPERS, *Pomegranate House*

2 sticks (1 cup) butter, room temperature
2 cups sugar
3 eggs
2 teaspoons almond extract
4 cups flour
1 tablespoon baking powder
¼ teaspoon cream of tartar
½ teaspoon salt
Red food coloring

GLAZE:
1 cup powdered sugar
1 tablespoon plus 2 teaspoons evaporated milk
½ teaspoon almond extract

In a large bowl, cream together butter and sugar. Add eggs, one at a time, mixing after each addition. Stir in almond extract. In a medium bowl, sift together flour, baking powder, cream of tartar and salt; add to butter mixture; stir to combine. Add a few drops of red food coloring to the dough and swirl through the mixture (do not over mix to retain a swirled batter). Cover and chill the dough for at least 1 hour, or until baking.

Preheat oven to 350°F. Roll chilled dough into balls and place 2 inches apart on a greased baking sheet. Flatten balls slightly. Bake for 10 minutes.

While cookies are baking, combine the glaze ingredients in a small bowl. Glaze cookies while warm.

BlissWood

Spend some time in a peaceful country setting amidst majestic live oaks in your choice of turn-of-the-century Texas cottages, completely furnished with antiques of their era—all on the Lehmann Legacy Ranch, a 650-acre working ranch only an hour west of Houston.

Animals abound on the ranch, including horses, Corriente cattle, llamas, camels, miniature donkeys, peacocks and even American bison. Relax with catch-and-release bass fishing in the ranch's stocked lakes.

INNKEEPERS:	Carol Davis
ADDRESS:	13251 Newberg Road, Cat Spring, Texas 78933
TELEPHONE:	(713) 301-3235
E-MAIL:	carol@blisswood.net
WEBSITE:	www.blisswood.net
ROOMS:	8 Cottages; Private baths
CHILDREN:	Call ahead
PETS:	Call ahead; Resident dogs

Alice's Cookie Surprise

Makes 4 to 5 Dozen Cookies

1 stick (½ cup) butter, room temperature
½ cup white sugar
½ cup packed brown sugar
1 egg
½ teaspoon vanilla extract (or more, to your taste)
1¾ cups flour
½ teaspoon salt
½ teaspoon baking soda
½ teaspoon cinnamon (or more, to your taste)
½ cup vegetable oil (such as canola)
2 cups crushed cornflakes
½ cup shredded coconut
½ cup finely chopped pecans

Preheat oven to 325°F. Beat together butter, white sugar and brown sugar in a large bowl until creamy. Add the egg and vanilla; beat well.

Sift together the flour, salt, baking soda and cinnamon. Add the flour mixture alternately with the oil to the butter mixture (start and end with the flour mixture), stirring well after each addition. Stir in the cornflakes, coconut and pecans.

Drop dough by heaping teaspoonfuls, 2 inches apart, onto an ungreased baking sheet. Bake for 8–12 minutes, until the cookies turn golden brown and achieve a moist, yet chewy consistency (these cookies bake quickly, so check for doneness after 8 minutes).

MANSION AT JUDGE'S HILL

Built in 1900, the historic Goodall Wooten House is now home to Austin's premier boutique hotel and fine dining restaurant. The re-invention of this architectural masterpiece has created a

plush haven where guests can retreat from the bustling streets of downtown Austin. The fine accommodations at the Mansion at Judges' Hill furnish all of the luxurious niceties necessary for a restful and carefree stay. The guest service staff is available twenty-four hours a day. Indulge in the in-room spa services. Take advantage of the business, laundry, and babysitting services. Complimentary parking, local newspapers, and day passes to a comprehensive local fitness facility are given to all overnight guests.

The elegant and refined Judges' Hill Restaurant offers an amazing culinary experience. Dine in the exquisite dining room, intimate lounge, or breezy veranda and delight in the seasonal menu blending fresh flavors from around the world. There are a plethora of choices on the ever-expanding wine list for a special libation to compliment your meal.

INNKEEPER:	Lisa Wiedemann
ADDRESS:	1900 Rio Grande, Austin, Texas 78705
TELEPHONE:	(512) 495-1800; (800) 311-1619; (512) 476-4769 fax
E-MAIL:	lisa@judgeshill.com
WEBSITE:	www.judgeshill.com
ROOMS:	48 Rooms; 2 Suites; Private Baths
CHILDREN:	Welcome
PETS:	Dogs and Cats welcome

Cranberry & White Chocolate Biscotti

Makes 2 Dozen Biscotti

1 stick (½ cup) butter, room temperature
1½ cups sugar
2 large eggs
½ teaspoon almond extract
2½ cups flour
1 teaspoon baking powder
½ teaspoon salt
1½ cups dried cranberries
1 egg white
6 (1-ounce) squares premium
   white chocolate (such as Lindt or Baker's)

Preheat oven to 350°F. Line a heavy, large baking sheet with parchment paper. In a large bowl, beat butter, sugar, eggs and almond extract with a mixer until well blended. Whisk together flour, baking powder and salt; stir into butter mixture until well combined. Stir in cranberries.

Divide dough in half. With floured hands, shape each half into a 2½ x 9½ x 1-inch long log. Transfer both logs to the baking sheet, spacing evenly (the logs will spread during baking). Whisk egg white in a small bowl until foamy. Brush egg white on top and sides of each log (this aids browning).

Bake for 35 minutes, or until golden brown. Leave logs on baking sheet; cool completely on a wire rack. Transfer logs to a cutting surface. Using a serrated knife, cut logs diagonally into ½-inch thick slices. Arrange slices, cut-side-down, on the baking sheet (without parchment this time). Bake for 10 minutes. Turn biscotti and bake until just beginning to color, about 5 minutes. Transfer biscotti to a wire rack and cool completely.

In a double boiler, over simmering water, melt white chocolate, stirring, until smooth. Using a fork, drizzle melted chocolate over biscotti. Let stand until chocolate sets, about 30 minutes, or refrigerate to speed the process. Store in an airtight container.

DECKER CREEK
BED & BREAKFAST & BISCUIT

"Our full name is Decker Creek Bed and Breakfast and Biscuit.
At Decker Creek, dogs are guests, too."
—INNKEEPERS, Decker Creek B&B&B

The Decker Creek cabin is just fifteen miles from Austin and was built in 2006 with dog guests in mind. There are wooden and tile floors, a fenced yard, screened porch, plus an outdoor dog wash area. Dog food bowls, dog sheets, blankets, and beds are provided inside the cabin. Homemade dog biscuits are prepared for the canine guests.

The human amenities at Decker Creek's cabin include large windows with views of the surrounding woods and meadows, a whirlpool tub in the living area, a kitchen, a comfy king or twin-size beds, and an outdoor grill. Dogs and their upright companions are free to romp the fifty acres of rural countryside intersected by Decker Creek. The full country breakfast is served, by prior arrangement, at a time that is convenient for the human guests. The huevos rancheros are made with farm-fresh eggs and the coffee is fabulous.

INNKEEPERS:	Pat and Byron Rathbun
ADDRESS:	16029 Decker Lake Road, Manor, Texas 78653
TELEPHONE:	(512) 743-8835; (512) 743-8090
E-MAIL:	pat.rathburn@gmail.com
WEBSITE:	www.deckercreek.com
ROOMS:	1 Cottage; Private bath
CHILDREN:	Welcome, if well behaved
PETS:	Dogs are welcome; resident dogs, a Lab and Aussie

Decker Creek Dog Biscuits

Number of Servings
(depends on the size of biscuits you make.)

*"The original recipe called for pumpkin,
but I use peanut butter instead, since it is easier
to keep on hand. Not only do our dogs love them—
the guest dogs have given very positive reviews!"*
—INNKEEPER, *Decker Creek Bed and Breakfast*

3 cups wheat flour
2 cups old-fashioned oats (not instant)
¼ cup milk powder
¼ cup wheat bran
½ teaspoon garlic powder
⅓ cup peanut butter (or pumpkin)
1 egg
1¼ cups water

Preheat oven to 275°F. In a big bowl, mix all the dry ingredients.
Add the wet ingredients and blend well together. Knead the mixture with your hands until the dough is stiff and not sticky. Roll it
out to cookie-cutter thickness; cut into any shapes you like. Place
biscuits on an ungreased cookie sheet. Bake at least 1½ hours—
and as much as 3 hours—if you want them really hard.

Geographical List of Inns

Alphabetical List of Inns

Recipe Index

Also Available from 3D Press

High Altitude Baking
$14.95 / 192 pages / ISBN 978-1-889593-15-9

The Bed & Breakfast Cookbook Series

New England Bed & Breakfast Cookbook
(CT, MA, ME, NH, RI, & VT)
$19.95 / 320 pages / ISBN 978-1-889593-12-8

North Carolina Bed & Breakfast Cookbook
$19.95 / 320 pages / ISBN 978-1-889593-08-1

Pennsylvania Bed & Breakfast Cookbook
$19.95 / 304 pages / ISBN 978-1-889593-18-0

Virginia Bed & Breakfast Cookbook
$19.95 / 320 pages / ISBN 978-1-889593-14-2

Washington State Bed & Breakfast Cookbook
$19.95 / 320 pages / ISBN 978-1-889593-05-0

New Titles in Spring and Summer 2008

Georgia Bed & Breakfast Cookbook
$19.95 / 320 pages / ISBN 978-1-889593-19-7

California Bed and Breakfast Cookbook
revised and updated
$19.95 / 328 pages / ISBN 978-1-889593-21-0

3D Press Order Form

3005 Center Green Drive, Suite 220 • Boulder CO 80301
800-258-5830 • www.bigearthpublishing.com

Please Send Me	Price	Quantity
Southern Church Suppers	$19.95	_____
High Altitude Baking	$14.95	_____
California Bed & Breakfast Cookbook *(available Summer 2008)*	$19.95	_____
Georgia Bed & Breakfast Cookbook *(available Summer 2008)*	$19.95	_____
New England Bed & Breakfast Cookbook	$19.95	_____
North Carolina Bed & Breakfast Cookbook	$19.95	_____
Pennsylvania Bed & Breakfast Cookbook	$19.95	_____
Texas Bed & Breakfast Cookbook	$19.95	_____
Virginia Bed & Breakfast Cookbook	$19.95	_____
Washington State Bed & Breakfast Cookbook	$19.95	_____

Subtotal $ _____

Add $5.00 shipping for 1st book add $1 for each additional book **$** _____

Total Enclosed $ _____

Send To

Name _____

Address _____

City /State/Zip _____

Phone _____ Gift from _____

We accept checks and money orders. Please make checks payable to Big Earth Publishing.

Please charge my   **VISA**   **MASTERCARD**   **AMEX**   **DISCOVER**

(circle one)

Card Number _____

Expiration Date _____